Empty Seats

Empty Seats

Wanda Adams Fischer

Empty Seats

Cover design by: Carol Coogan
Website: www.carolcoogandesign.com
Typeset by: Medlar Publishing Solutions Pvt Ltd., India
Cover photo of the author by Franco Vogt
www.francovogt.com
Distributed by Epigraph Publishing Service

ISBN: 978-0-9995049-0-1

Library of Congress Control Number: 2017916246

Dedication

*This book is dedicated to Jack Lanzillotti, who made it to the big
leagues as a producer and Emmy Award winner but whose young life was cut way
too short,
and to four of my favorite players who are no longer with us:
Tony Conigliaro, Harmon Killebrew, Dick Radatz and Kirby Puckett.
They remain part of my life.
Every day.*

Table of Contents

The Roster

Pitchers

James (Jimmy) Bailey (#11) (R), Weymouth, Massachusetts
Cameron "Bud" Prescott (#32) R), Athens, Georgia
Alex Gibson (#24) (L), St. Louis, Missouri
Marion McGhee (#37) (L), Missoula, Montana
Richie Newman (#14) (R), Whittier, California
Jerry Malone (#33) (R), Natchez, Mississippi
Robert Mangino (#15) (R), Yonkers, New York
John Jordan (#17) (L), Kingsport, Tennessee
Joey Lincoln (#22) (R), Roanoke, Virginia
Johnny Duncan (#21) (R), Sandusky, Ohio
Julio Nieves (#19) (L), Ciudad Juarez, Mexico
Alan Petrie (#26) (R), Seattle, Washington
Andy McManus (#12) (L), Skowhegan, Maine

Catchers

Russell Brindisi (#7) (R), Trenton, New Jersey
Johnny Forsythe (#10) (R), Birmingham, Alabama
Stevie Long (#27) (R), Utica, New York

Infielders

Tommy Fitzpatrick (#20) (R), Geneva, Illinois
Nick Golden (#9) (L), Maryville, Tennessee
Billy Randall (#8) (R), Greeneville, South Carolina

Joey Tidwell (#5) (R), Gainesville, Florida
Doug Tremaine (#16) (R), Tucson, Arizona
Al Logan (#18) (R), San Diego, California
Mike McKinney (#28) (R), Renkin, Georgia

Outfielders

Donnie Jefferson (#23) (R), Gary, Indiana
Dave Arroyo (#2) (L), Ponce, Puerto Rico
Jack Milkewicz (#4) (R), Port Huron, Michigan
Tommy Colucci (#3) (R), Kenmore, New York
Tim Jakobowski (#30) (L), Troy, New York
Jamie Kirk (#31) (R), Houston, Texas
Davey Alvarez (#28) (R), San Antonio, Texas

Management Team

General Manager: Skip Trainor
Bench Coach: Finn Jackson
Pitching Coach: Cesar Dominguez
Hitting Coach: Mick "The Stick" McDonald
First Base Coach: Joey Tagliaria
Third Base Coach: Frankie Adams

CHAPTER 1

Two Jimmys

Neatsfoot oil, as my father worked it into my glove, smelled like an old, greasy body shop. He said it was the only way to get rid of the creaks it picked up over the long Massachusetts winter.

I was about four years old the spring my father took me out to the yard, a baseball in one hand, and two leather baseball gloves–one very worn, the other very small and very new, in the other.

My father looked like a giant to me. He was a little over six feet tall with broad shoulders. Whenever he looked at a baseball, his wry smile showed his crooked front teeth, yellowed from many years of drinking coffee. He was only in his mid-thirties, but wrinkles encased his eyes from so many years of squinting at the sun. He was the handsome man who still made my mother giggle whenever he walked by and patted her on the rear. Under the wear and tear was a spark, an energy I knew nothing about.

When we went out in the backyard to play ball, he wore the clothes from under his shipyard overhauls—worn, faded blue jeans with frayed cuffs, a worn white t-shirt, white socks and his steel-toed safety boots. He looked happy and comfortable.

But he looked especially happy when he had a baseball in his hand.

He lifted the two gloves in his hand, holding them as if they were the World Series trophy.

The older glove needed new stitching between the thumb and the forefinger. It had a lot of mileage between the palm and where the hand entered the leather for protection. Written in heavy black pen, but barely visible, was the name *Jimmy B.* Short for James Bailey.

The smaller glove was the color of gold April sunshine, with its brand new stitching, stiff palm and shape. Inside, my father wrote: *Jimmy B Jr.*

"This glove needs some work," Dad counseled. "Here's how we're going to do it. We have this oil we have to work into it, and then we're going to throw the ball around. When we're done, we're going to put the ball inside the pocket of the glove and wrap it in elastics. We'll leave it that way for a few days and see what happens."

Dad worked in the shipyard, so his huge, calloused fingers were strong and did the work of an impact wrench on the leather. Round and round he rubbed the oil, until the glove changed from its sunny color to a deep earth tone.

"That should do it for now. Here. This is yours now," he said.

Mine? Really? A glove of my own?

I tried to put the glove on my right hand. It fit me like an overgrown snow mitten. Backwards.

"No, no," dad laughed. "You're a righty. That means the glove goes on the left hand. You throw with your right hand, you catch with your left. See?"

He put his own glove on his left hand to demonstrate.

I nodded in awe.

He stood back about two feet from me and threw the hard baseball to me.

I didn't catch it. He showed me how to cradle the glove, then tossed it again gently.

I dropped the ball and started to cry.

"Don't worry, son," he assured me, "it will come."

We went out just about every night after dinner. It didn't matter that he had come home tired after working overtime at the shipyard and just wanted to relax, read the newspaper or catch up on how the Red Sox did that afternoon. Playing catch was a priority, between me and my dad. My sisters had to do something with our mother, and I liked it that way.

In 1945, right after World War II ended, my father had been a top prospect in the St. Louis Cardinal organization. He wanted to be with the Red Sox, his hometown team, but it was the Cards who picked him. So he worked his way up through the ranks. Single A. Double A. Triple A. In Triple A, he pitched a no-hitter, and he was cruising. He figured he was "this close" to being called up to the majors, to "The Show." He didn't smoke, drink, or chase women; instead, he worked on perfecting his pitches.

During the off-season in those days, major league players usually had to take other jobs to pay the bills, like selling cars or insurance.

Some of them, like my dad, worked in a shipyard.

That's where he met the gorgeous blonde knockout, Mary Simmons, the one he called "The Filly." She was a secretary in the main office, and once he caught a glimpse of her, he was smitten.

She looked like the pin-up girls whose photos graced airplanes and ship lockers during World War II. She was over six feet tall. When she walked down the street, both men and women were stunned by her height, and turned to take in her beauty and grace. She pinned her ash-blond hair up on top of her head so it fell down in soft ringlets, which she then secured with hidden bobby pins, accentuating her steel-gray eyes. Her make-up was always perfect—with just the right touch of foundation and perfectly blended rouge on her cheeks. Her lipstick was always fresh. She could have been on the cover of any magazine, without even the slightest touch-up from a professional cosmetologist.

The first time she noticed my father, he was walking down the road to the main entrance of the shipyard, lunchbox in hand, and she wanted to know who he was. She asked one of her co-workers, and found out that he was a baseball player. "Minor leagues, somewhere," they said.

"He's kinda cute," she mused.

"Mary, these guys are a dime a dozen," her supervisor said, walking away.

"Kinda cute" meant he was tall with a ruddy complexion from playing ball in the sun. His short-cropped sandy-brown hair framed his face, revealing high cheekbones under slightly rounded cheeks. He had a boyish look for someone who walked with a confident, masculine air. She guessed that hiding underneath those work clothes was a muscular, virile physique.

She decided she'd find out who he was and where he played ball. She didn't like baseball, or know anything about it. But she'd learn.

She went to the ballpark to watch him pitch. Her knowledge about the sport didn't grow, but her crush on Jimmy did. She wore her most stylish hats and high-heels, crossing her elegant legs while she cheered his every pitch. When he wasn't pitching, she paid no attention to the game; instead she filed her nails or primped her hair.

She saw a cadre of young women throw themselves at the ballplayers, particularly in the bullpen. She looked down her nose at them. "Cheap and disgusting," she thought. "They wear dime store makeup and it looks tawdry. Their skirts are way too short. And they wear sleeveless shirts. Sleeveless! My mother would never let me out of the house in a sleeveless shirt!"

The boys in the bullpen ate it up. They whistled and hooted at those girls from the bullpen bench. Mary made the Sign of The Cross and called on the Virgin Mary to save the souls of those vixens. "Boys will be boys," she thought, "but girls should know better."

Although she trusted her Jimmy not to react to "those girls," she knew what a temptation they could be. She knew some of the bullpen boys left the ballpark with one of those women on his arm, heading toward some rundown hotel for a temporary tryst, and bullpen bragging rights for the next day.

In 1948, she saw Jim's second no-hitter. Without the walk he gave up in the top of the ninth, it would have been a perfect game. But she still didn't know how important that was.

The next day, he asked her to marry him. She was coy about it for five minutes, then turned around, lifted her wide-brimmed hat, batted her eyelashes at him, and said yes. They were married two months later, in a small service at a Catholic church. She carried yellow roses and wore a tea-length pale yellow dress that she already owned. It was almost white. She wished she could afford a new white dress, but this was nice, too. Anything she wore was stunning, he thought. Only a few people were there, but it was a nice wedding for them. Afterwards, they went into the church basement for punch and cookies.

In the back of her mind, Mary knew the day could come when he might get the chance to play in the major leagues, when he'd be traveling across the country, exposed to all those temptations, all those scantily-clad, over-made-up girls who stalked baseball players looking for a quick romance with someone who might become famous one day. The thought haunted her to the point of obsession. She would not allow it. No. She would not let him go into the majors. What was more important to him? Baseball or her?

Soon she hated the smell of anything that even remotely resembled leather—new boots, a wallet—anything that might remind her of a baseball glove. The sight of any uniform with a number on the back made her anxious. It didn't matter if it was a football jersey or an employee of the gas company.

That spring, just before 1949 baseball season, my big sister Debbie was born. At the end of April, my dad got the call, up to the bigs. They offered him $5,000.

He went running home to The Filly and their four-week-old baby.

"Mary! Mary! They want me to pitch in the majors!" he screamed. He woke up the baby.

The Filly hadn't slept in a couple of days. She was not amused. "You cannot be serious," she said. "You don't mean that you would be leaving me here alone with this baby, do you, Jimmy?"

"But it's the chance of a lifetime," he insisted. "They asked me to join…"

She cut him off. "This baseball thing…Is it more important than your family? I mean, is it more important than me?" She looked at him with her soulful Ava Gardner eyes.

"No…It's not more important than you or the baby or family…It's just… It's just that it's what I've always dreamed about, and I don't know if the chance will come again," he said. "They offered me $5,000, Mary. I could only make $3,000 as a full-time worker at the shipyard. Think of it: Five thousand dollars!"

"What if you get hurt? What if you run off with one of those floozies? What good would that $5,000 do me then? I'd be all alone with this baby and you'd be running free."

His eyes pleaded with hers. She was not budging. The sleep deprivation was battling with his yearning desire to be a major league ballplayer.

"Well, I have one thing to say," she insisted. "If you go to St. Louis, don't come back. It's the Cardinals or me."

"What? Are you giving me an ultimatum?" he asked.

"Yes. That's what this is," she said. "An ultimatum."

He went out behind their tiny house and paced back and forth.

How can she do this to me? She knows how much this means to me! She knows how hard I have worked for this! How can she ask me to give up this dream? I got through being on a destroyer in the Pacific during the war, knowing I could come back to baseball. Now she wants me to give it all up? I love her so much. So much. But baseball is what I do. How can I give up one for the other?

The tug of war went on for two or three days. But she wouldn't give an inch.

Finally, he acquiesced. "Okay," he said. "I won't go to St. Louis."

Soon after, the Cardinals dropped him completely. So now, instead of working at the shipyard during the winter months, he worked there full time.

My other sister, Donna, was born two years later, and then me, in 1954.

Finally he had his boy. He could teach him all he knew about baseball.

From the day he handed me my glove and the can of neatsfoot oil, he taught me all his pitches, his tricks, his mental exercises, his warm-ups. I was his blank canvas, his Jimmy B, Jr.

When I was six years old, I tried out for Little League baseball. I could throw strikes even then. All the Little League coaches wanted me on their teams.

Not good enough for dad. He started his own team.

Dad had a knack for finding talent, whether it was hitting, pitching, throwing, catching, or running. He looked at my friends to see who had talent and he snagged them for his team.

And every night, he took me to the backyard to play catch. He put down a pitching rubber and a plate, and he expected me to throw from the pitching rubber to him over the plate. He called balls and strikes. It was easy for me to follow his directions.

We were winners. Statewide Little League champions. Pitcher of the year by the age of 12, then 13, then 14. High school pitcher of the year at 15, 16, 17, 18.

"Jimmy B, Jr. looks a lot like his dad," the newspapers declared.

"He could be the second coming of what his father might have been, had he not quit baseball abruptly," said a radio commentator.

I was the new king of the hill in my town. Everybody knew me as I walked down the street. I liked being a celebrity.

I came home from school one day after turning 18, and found a bunch of reporters surrounding my house. Dad was waiting for me at the door. A scout for the Montreal Expos had come to the house, contract in hand, to make an offer.

My dad was walking on air. The Filly was in the kitchen, crying. I thought of the most adult thing to say to the scout, without spilling my guts to him.

"I....I...I have to be concerned with the high school championship first," I stammered.

"Of course you do, Jimmy, of course you do. We wouldn't want it any other way," he responded, as he reached out his large calloused right hand to congratulate me. It seemed as if he and my dad had already worked out the whole thing. The Filly was having none of it.

"He's too young for this, James!" she protested to my dad. "He can't go on the road all alone! He's too young! He should go to college or something. He needs to stay with me!"

"Oh, come on, Mary," Dad insisted. "I've taught him everything I know. He's amazing. A great student. Now it's time for him to go with the professionals who can take him to the next level."

My sisters, with hands folded across their chests, snickered in the corner of the kitchen. Debbie, who was almost as tall me, and as gorgeous as The Filly herself, whispered into our younger sister's ear. They started to giggle, but covered their mouths so they wouldn't laugh out loud in front of The Expos scout.

"I see we may have a difference of opinion here," said the scout. "I'll go speak to his high school coach for a while. I'm supposed to meet with him today anyway. I'll be back later, after you folks have had some time to work this out."

He went out the door, put on his cap, and addressed the crowd of reporters still waiting on the lawn. "Not much to say right now, boys," he told them, as he got into his car and drove away.

Dad and The Filly went back and forth for a few hours.

Finally, The Filly gave up. "But YOU will be responsible if anything goes wrong!" she promised Dad.

"Nothing will go wrong. He will be supervised and taken care of," Dad insisted. "It's not like in the old days."

The scout returned with my high school coach. The reporters were gone by then. Dad and I met with them and signed the contract offer. The Filly stayed in the kitchen and refused to acknowledge the event.

Debbie said she hoped I would introduce her to some handsome baseball players when I made it to the major leagues. My younger sister Donna rolled her eyes, went to the fridge and picked out a Coca-Cola, flipped the cap off of the bottle, and went upstairs.

The story hit the newspapers. My ego grew exponentially with the recognition of my name and face by others. Girls were impressed and their boyfriends were jealous of me.

I pictured my name on a plaque at the Hall of Fame in Cooperstown. I'd show The Filly that baseball could be a life. It would be baseball for me. Baseball forever.

When I walked across the stage at graduation, in the spring of 1972, I felt relief. I could leave this podunk town and get on with the business of baseball.

But my podunk town was a bustling metropolis compared to where The Expos sent me to play Single-A ball.

After an endless drive across Massachusetts and New York state, Dad and The Filly dropped me off in Jamestown, New York at the home of the family with whom I'd be staying.

Jamestown, New York. Hometown of Lucille Ball, its only claim to fame. I was certain I could pitch my way from Jamestown to AA ball quickly and painlessly.

Players roomed with families instead of staying at hotels, it was cheaper and a better transition for the younger players away from their own families for the first time. Some players who came from other countries didn't speak English, so it helped them, too.

We looked around the neighborhood. The houses were close together, and didn't have driveways. Everyone parked on the street, which had an island down the center. The neighbors had planted some flowers on the island, which The Filly called, "very home-like."

My father just grunted. Maybe it brought back memories of his time in Single-A ball. He never talked about that time, before the war, even when we'd thrown the ball to each other in the backyard, all those nights.

There it was, 1048 Maryland Avenue, Jamestown. Dad pulled over and parked. We made our way up the narrow concrete walk and rang the doorbell.

"Mrs. Anderson?" Dad checked with the woman who answered the door. "I am bringing my son here because he's supposed to stay with you during baseball season."

"Oh, yes! Come in, come in!" she said. "My husband and son aren't home right now. I'm expecting them soon. Have a seat here in the parlor. Can I get you anything?"

"Well, I'd like a cup of coffee, if it wouldn't be too much trouble," The Filly said. "Jim, would you like something?"

"Coffee would be fine," Dad said.

"And Jimmy—can I call you Jimmy? Can I get you a pop?" Mrs. Anderson asked.

"A what?" I said.

"A pop—a Pepsi or a Coke?" she replied.

Where I come from, we call those things tonic, but I figured the learning had begun.

"Sure," I said. "Whatever you have."

Mrs. Anderson swept off to the kitchen.

"Nice place," Dad said. "Homey."

"I don't like leaving him," said The Filly. "I don't care how nice this is. But you're right, the house is pleasant, and Mrs. Anderson seems nice enough."

Nice. Nice. They kept using that word. I was tired from the ride, and I didn't know what to think.

Mrs. Anderson returned with three cups of coffee, a fancy creamer, a bowl of sugar, and a glass of "pop," on a tray she placed on a weathered oak coffee table.

"I guess that's why they call them coffee tables," she said.

After a short silence, my dad started the questions.

How far is it from here to the ball park? Is there a grocery store nearby? If we come to watch a game, is there a good restaurant that won't be too expensive? Where is the nearest Catholic church?

Oh, great, he *had* to ask the church question. Now she's going to think I need to go to church every day.

As Mrs. Anderson began to respond to the quiz, her husband and son walked in.

Bill Anderson was in his mid-forties, with a full head of brown hair, graying at the sides. He was shorter than me, thin and wiry. He looked like he might be a recreational runner. Their son, Paul, was about half a foot taller than his dad, also with brown hair, and more muscular than his father. He might be more inclined to be a football player. He was a year older than me and had a job at a local supermarket.

Mr. Anderson gave us a tour of the house. We all went to the bungalow's second floor, where three neat bedrooms were laid out around one bathroom.

"I wish we had more than one bathroom," Mr. Anderson said. "But this is it!" He walked us to the smallest of the three bedrooms and said, "Jimmy, this one will be yours while you're staying with us."

I had expected I'd be getting a girly room—their daughter had vacated it—but this room was actually nice. There was that word again.

A double bed, an empty dresser, a window looking out to the backyard, and a small but adequate closet. The woodwork was dark oak, matching the hardwood floors. Next to the bed was a dark maroon scatter rug. Mrs. Anderson said, "I put the rug by your bed so you wouldn't have cold feet in the morning. Sometimes, even in the summer, it can be cold around here."

That's something The Filly would think of. I looked over at The Filly. She seemed mildly pleased.

Dad and The Filly stayed in a hotel that night, while I nestled into the room. Paul Anderson gave me the once-over, muttering, "We'll talk," and went to his own room.

Sunshine pouring through the window woke me up early the first morning. *I'll have to do something about that. It's entirely too early to be getting up.* It was 5:45. I rolled over and pulled the covers and the pillow over my head. No rising and shining for me.

I thought about my sisters and the guys I'd played ball with at home. I was the only one drafted into the pros. Once that happened, they all stopped talking to me. I became untouchable. Debbie and Donna had friends who looked at me in awe, as if I was the second coming of Bill Monbouquette or Dick Radatz or something. That felt weird to me.

I never had a girlfriend in high school. I was too busy playing ball and trying to keep up my grades. I went to the prom with Cindy Stevens from up the street, and we had a great time, but it was nothing serious.

Mostly, I would miss my sisters. Even though I was a pain in the neck to them, and they were to me, I could always talk to them when I was confused.

And The Filly…Man, I knew I'd miss my mother's home cooking. She had kept me fed and ready to play ball for all these years. How was I going to stay at the top of my game without her food?

CHAPTER 2

First Day at Jamestown Stadium

I take a quick shower and grab some cereal in the kitchen, before hearing a familiar horn outside at 8:30 the first morning in Jamestown.

It's Dad and The Filly, here to drive me to the ball park for my first workout with the team.

Dad wants to meet the coach. After all, he had been my coach basically since I had been born, so why would I expect anything else? He's been my guardian angel of baseball since I was just a toddler, since that first time in the backyard. He's handing the torch over to someone new. He wants to make sure the transition is solid. He wants to shake the hand of the man who's going to take his place. He wants to have confidence in the new "him." I can accept that. Change isn't easy for him.

Paul sits at the breakfast nook and looks at me. I roll my eyes back at him, like a good embarrassed teenaged comrade would. He responds with a wry smile.

I say a quick goodbye to Mrs. Anderson and run out to the car.

"How'd you sleep last night?" The Filly asks.

"Fine, Ma, fine. I woke up early. I'm a little nervous about starting with the team."

"You'll be okay," Dad says. "I want to size up this ball park, though."

"I figured...I don't have to be there until ten, according to the papers I got from the home club," I remind him.

"Son, you need to learn—never be late for anything when it comes to baseball! Never, ever! If you're early, it makes an impression," Dad says. "That's cardinal rule number one."

"I'm not playing for the Cardinals," I joke, trying to lighten his mood.

"That's not funny!" he snaps. "Baseball is serious business. You need to learn that. You need to listen and learn. You're going to have to listen to the coach and everyone associated with the club. That's how you get better. You think you know everything? You're at the bottom rung on the ladder."

Oh yeah? I'll show them what I already know! If they didn't think I knew how to play ball, why did they sign me? Why would they even invite me to come to this god-forsaken place? Jamestown, New York might as well be Timbuktu. The only reason I'm here is to play ball!

"Ok, Dad, I read you, loud and clear," I say. "Loud and clear." I feel like I'm about two again, sinking into the chair. My shoulders droop and my confidence goes south. I wonder if I'll even reach six feet again by the time we get to the ballpark.

"Now, where are those directions to the baseball field?" asks The Filly. "Oh, here they are, in my pocketbook. Yes—Jim—take that next left and we should be very close."

Dad approaches the street with caution, which is certainly not the way he drives in Boston. He steers the huge station wagon to a parking lot at the end of a dead-end street.

There it is: Jamestown Stadium, where I would be making my pitching debut as a member of the Single-A Jamestown Falcons, affiliated with the Montreal Expos.

The structure looms large from the parking lot, but I had pitched at bigger places. One of the championship games my team had played took place in McCoy Stadium in Pawtucket, which is the home of the AAA Pawtucket Red Sox.

And I got to throw batting practice at Fenway Park once, when there were a number of scouts in the area. But that wasn't the same as pitching in an actual game. It was daunting to step on the mound where Bill Monbouquette and Dick Radatz had pitched, but without batters and runners to worry about, it seemed too easy.

Jamestown Stadium seats about 3,000 fans. Straightaway centerfield is about 410 feet from home plate, so batters need a good crack of the bat to make it over the fence. Left field is a little shorter, at 335 feet, and right field is at 342, so left-handed batters could hit home runs over the right-field fence a little easier. All have short porches, meaning the fences aren't too high, not like the Green Monster at Fenway Park.

My dad has schooled me on all this. He did his research at the Tufts Library in North Weymouth weeks ago.

The place is deserted.

"Let's walk around the park," Dad says.

The Filly stays in the car.

Dad and I start walking around the outside of the stadium, in silence. He kicks up bits of dirt as he walks. His clunky work boots make small clouds of tiny pebbles and soot puff around him.

"Son, this is your big opportunity. Don't blow it. You've worked hard to get here. It's very easy to get caught up in things when you're away from home, away from the comforts you've known in your short life. You're a good kid, but you're not immune to the world. I don't know what else to say, except I'm proud of what you've done to get here. I know you've got what it takes to go further. And I know you could lose everything if you're not careful."

What the heck is he talking about? Careful about what?

"I'm not sure what you mean," I reply, "but I'll keep my eyes and ears open. I promise."

"That's all I can ask for," he says.

"Okay."

"Okay." And he smiles back at me with a grin that I don't see much these days.

He's so tired when he comes home from working at the shipyard, and then running to make it to my baseball games, and then re-hashing what I did right and wrong at the games, I've rarely seen anything make him happy.

Today was different.

Members of the team start trickling in. They come in all shapes and sizes, from all over the country and the world. Mexico. The Dominican Republic. Venezuela. But from where I sit, even Texas is another part of the world. I can't understand a word that comes out the mouths of those guys from the south.

Skip Trainor, our manager, is a retired major league ballplayer who had to stop playing when he broke his leg sliding into a particularly stubborn catcher. He likes to tell people that the catcher broke his ankle in the process, and he never got involved in baseball again.

"Too stupid to manage," he'd say. "Too dumb to get out of my way. Should've been a sign."

Skip has a wad of chew packed strategically in his cheek. My dad says this is typical of big leaguers. To me, the stuff is gross.

Skip has a huge gut that hangs over his uniform. It swallows his belt and makes his legs look so skinny that I wonder why it took so long for his leg to break while he was playing. He wears Coke-bottle-thick eyeglasses under his ball cap and latches onto an ever-present clipboard with unreadable notes all over the pages.

Skip wants everyone to think he's mean. I see through this.

His managerial staff are other old Major League ballplayers—none of whose names would mean anything to an average fan.

Finn Jackson is the bench coach. He was a utility infielder who once hit .301 during one season for the Kansas City Athletics, before they moved to Oakland. Somehow, he lost favor with Athletics owner Charlie Finley, who dropped him from the team, and no one else wanted him. He's Skip's right-hand man now.

Joey Tagliaria coaches first base. Rumor has it when he played in the majors for the Cincinnati Reds, he was a hot-tempered catcher who was often thrown out of games for arguing balls and strikes with umpires. He was good at gunning down runners who were trying to steal second base on the Reds' pitchers, but then he would gloat at the batter the next time he came up to bat, often leading to on-and off-field conflicts. My dad says he calmed down considerably after his wife left him a few years ago.

Frankie Adams coaches third base, and I've heard that he's the kindest person on this entire team. He will counsel new players with sage advice, but expects them to listen to him. He's not happy when a guy seeks his wisdom and then ignores it.

Hitting coach is Mick "The Stick" McDonald. He was once a legendary hitter for the Detroit Tigers system, hitting 40 home runs every year—until he found out, during the offseason, that he loved beer and whisky more than he loved sending the ball over the fence. Someone said he could have been on his way to the Hall of Fame if he'd quit the booze.

And the guy I will be working with—the pitching coach, Cesar Dominguez—was once a teammate of the great Bob Gibson on the St. Louis Cardinals. I cannot lie—I hated the Cardinals when they beat the Red Sox in seven games in 1967, but the it was an amazing series, great for baseball.

He's from the Dominican Republic and is a true gentleman and a scholar of baseball. He watches every move every young pitcher makes, and then says, in Spanish, *"Viene aqui,"* then realizes that he has spoken in Spanish, and says, "Come here, *hijo*." Then he explains which subtle tweaks need to be made in delivery or hand position. If the pitcher cannot make the adjustment almost immediately, Cesar gets after him more.

Skip calls the entire team, along with the coaches, out to the field.

Most of us are new—recent high school graduates, newly signed to the team. Some, though, had been here before, trying to get out of Single-A ball up to Double-A, but were not promoted. They're not happy to be here. But I am.

"So here we all are," says Skip. "We are a motley crew! That doesn't mean we won't become a team. That's the goal—to become a team."

"Yeah, yeah," says this guy next to me, #15. He was here last year and didn't get called up. "I've heard this one before."

Skip introduces the coaching staff and breaks us up into units. Pitchers go with Dominguez, hitters with McDonald, and the rest are split up among the other coaches to take infield or outfield practice, or run sprints.

Dominguez brings the pitchers together. I notice that #15 is looking in on at what's happening with the rest of us. I'm sure he's thinking, "These skinny, wet-behind-the-ears guys are my competition? No sweat!" And some of us are thinking, "He must be a loser, if he wasn't sent up after a year here!"

"*Escúchame, por favor!* Listen up, please," says Dominguez. "*Tenemos mucho trabajo hacer.* We have a lot of work to do." He explains that he is speaking in both Spanish and English because we have one pitcher who is from Mexico, and his English isn't too good. "I hope you will help him as he learns to speak *en ingles*," he says.

He sends us out to do sprints, followed by warm-up exercises. As we're doing stretches and leg lifts, the guy next to me, #32, asks in a thick southern drawl, "Hey, where'd you come here from?"

"Eastern Massachusetts," I reply. "Little town called Weymouth, about 15 miles south of Boston."

"Oh, Red Sox country," he says. "Do you say 'cah' and 'Hah-vahd Yahd,' too?"

"I suppose you'd think that," I reply. "It's how we talk."

"Yup," he chuckles. "You prob'ly think I sound like good ole General Robert E. Lee!"

"Maybe," I say cautiously, "But I really haven't met too many people from the south. My sister's friend's father is from Virginia, and I know him, but that's about it."

"Well, we'll have to translate for each other," he says. "The name's Bud Prescott. I'm from Athens, Georgia, just outside Atlanta."

"Jimmy…Jimmy Bailey," I reply.

"Pleased to meet you, Jimmy. I feel a long way from home," Bud says.

"I feel like I'm on the other side of the moon," I tell him.

"Yup, that's what it feels like, doesn't it?" Bud says. "Guess the object is to make sure the hitters we face don't send the ball to the other side of the moon!"

I like this guy.

I remain wary of #15.

CHAPTER 3

#15

Bobby Mangino had swagger without the charm. His ragged personality was shaped on the streets of his Yonkers neighborhood.

He was a little over six feet tall, with olive skin and black curly hair that stuck out every which way from underneath his ball cap. If his long hair made him look like a hippie, that wasn't his aim. He just didn't care enough to tame it.

Now in his second year as a pitcher in Single-A ball, he wasn't happy when the parent club told him he wasn't being promoted to Double-A. He took several bats to the benches, lockers, and walls inside the clubhouse, which almost got him thrown out of the club altogether.

But Skip sat him down and convinced him—or thought he did—that it wasn't a "death sentence," that he had talent, that if he worked hard during the off season, he could probably be promoted in mid-season to Double-A. Besides, Skip said, if his ERA improved, or if one of the Double-A pitchers became injured, Bobby would certainly be called up.

Bobby spent much of the off season sulking in the room he shared at home with his ten-year-old brother, Charlie, in a grungy Yonkers seventh-floor walk-up, surrounded by screeching brake sounds, horns and sirens.

Bobby hated the place. He hated Charlie, the little weasel who was always underfoot. He hated his mother, who doted on him when he played Little League, Babe Ruth and then high school baseball.

"There's MY Bobby!" she'd preen. "See how great he is? He's going to play for the New York Yankees *someday*. The New York Yankees! Just like Mickey Mantle!"

So, the day the Montreal Expos signed him, instead of the Yankees, his mother went into the bathroom and slammed the door. He could hear her crying, even though she started the shower running to try to hide the noise. He heard her slamming things around in the bathroom. She did this for more than an hour. Charlie was running around the small, cramped living room, while Bobby and his high school coach spoke to the scout from The Expos, who explained that he would be going to Jamestown, New York, to play Single-A ball that summer.

Jamestown, freakin' New York? Where the hell is that? I've never been north of Dobbs Ferry! Is Jamestown on the Hudson River? Holy crap!

When the scout handed Bobby a check for $15,000 to cover his signing bonus, he knew it would mean one thing: His father would make a cameo appearance to get his share.

The elder Robert Mangino was rarely in either of his sons' lives. He only showed up when he needed money, and his ex-wife hardly ever had any to spare. When he read in *The New York Post* that Robert Mangino, Jr. of Yonkers High School was being signed by The Montreal Expos, he was most certainly interested.

Bobby was 18 by that time, though, and it was truly *his* money, not his mother's, not his father's. He told his coach he wanted to find a bank where he could open an account, not a joint account with one of his parents.

The coach didn't think this was a good idea.

"Bobby," his coach said, "what happens if you are up in Jamestown and you need some money? If you don't have a joint account, no one will be able to get it for you."

"That's the point, coach," he replied. "I don't want anyone else to get it. Ever. I'll get by when I'm up there. It's the boondocks, right? And I'll be staying with a family, so I won't need much money. I'll be getting a small paycheck, too."

"Okay. If that's what you want. Let's go do it."

On their way out of the building, as they were walking down the stairs, there he was: Robert Mangino, Sr.

"Where's my money?" he asked Bobby. "I deserve at least half. I'm half of you."

The coach tried to intervene. "The Expos haven't sent the money yet," he fibbed.

The coach found himself shoved back against the wall. "That's not how these things work," insisted the elder Mangino. "I know you've got it. Hand it over."

"No!" Bobby said. "It's MINE. I worked for it. Where the hell were you when I was playing ball to get this? Where the hell were you when Ma was working nights so that she could come to my games? Where the hell were you? I never looked up from the pitcher's mound and saw your ugly face! You deserve half? For what?"

"You wouldn't be standing here if it wasn't for me!" Robert Mangino said.

"For a sperm donation? Because you beat mom up and made her have sex? You think I don't know how you operate? I watched when you forced yourself on her when she got pregnant with Charlie—a night I'll never forget!"

The coach stayed out of the argument. He began to understand the Bobby he'd seen while serving as the boy's mentor.

"Don't you speak to me like that!" Robert Mangino said. "I'm your father!"

"Really? When have you ever acted like a father, a real dad?" Bobby asked.

"You don't know what you're talking about," Robert Mangino said. "You're an asshole. You're feeling your oats because now you're mister major-leaguer. Let me tell you…"

"You can't tell me nothing,'" interrupted Bobby. "I've seen it all myself. I ain't stupid. I ain't blind. I can see a fastball comin' at me at 90 miles an hour. You think I can't see what you've done?"

His father grabbed his arm and slapped his face. "Don't you ever, ever talk to me like that again!"

"Like what? Like telling the truth?" Bobby asked. "No, you ain't gettin' nothin' that I've earned. I'm not Ma. You can't sweet talk me."

His father slammed him against the hallway wall, holding both of his shoulders against the filthy cinder blocks. "You don't know who you're dis-respecting, so you need to keep your mouth shut," he said. "You think you're such big stuff today. You just wait. You just wait."

Off he went.

The coach stepped forward. "You alright?" he asked.

"Yeah," Bobby said. "Just want to get this check into the bank."

I hate him. I hate him. I hate him more than I can say. He hurt my ma. All she did was try to keep us all together. He's a sleaze bag. He don't know nothin' about being a father. He's my dad, he says. He says he's owed half of this money! Ha! This is MY money! No sleaze bag fake dad is going to squeeze a penny out of me. No. No. I hate him. I HATE HIM.

After he and the coach had safely put the check into a bank account, Bobby went back to his room and pounded his fist into his pillow on the bed, so hard it hurt his hand. Then he buried his face into the smashed-up pillow and—cried, while trying to hide from his little brother.

He muttered, "I hate him, I hate him, I HATE HIM!" over and over again into his pillow, until he slipped into a deep sleep.

CHAPTER 4

Bud Prescott

The pride of Athens, Georgia, Cameron Cheslee "Bud" Prescott was tall, blonde, blue-eyed, and square-jawed. Bud was the ballplayer on his high school team who was the Pied Piper to the girls. They adored his sly smile and overall movie star looks.

He didn't understand the attention; he just loved the game, and he could play for hours on end. He could get up at six in the morning, take the field, shag balls while batters sprayed pepper all over the outfield, take batting practice for hours, do fielding drills, all until the sun went down. He would forget to eat. His coaches had to remind him to drink water.

Girls would be waiting for him to come off the field. *"Oooohhhh, Bud!"* they'd squeal, *"Can we go to the Krystal and get a burger? Our treat!"*

He'd say, "I need to go home and clean up. My mom has dinner waiting for me," as he got into the 1971 Plymouth Barracuda his grandmother bought him.

Bud's home was an ante-bellum, four-columned white house, straight out of the set of *Gone with the Wind*.

This was the only house, the only life, that Bud had known. His mother, Rebecca Caldwell Prescott, whose grandfather had been a prominent slave owner in the area, was active in the local chapter of the Daughters of the Confederacy. A debutante at age 18, she was presented at an elegant cotillion dance by her father, Josiah Caldwell, Jr., who beamed with pride as they walked down the thirty-foot-wide, sweeping staircase of the Delta Delta Delta sorority house at the University of Georgia.

Rebecca was a stunning beauty, a Georgia peach, whose classic looks were only outdone by her charm and wit. She had many suitors and, just like her son, Bud, could have chosen anyone from the crowd who followed her everywhere.

She only had eyes for Cheslee Prescott.

Cheslee James Prescott was mysterious. He lived in that stunning columned house with his mother, the renowned landowner and widow Maude Ewell Prescott. He was devoted to his mother, but he was also his own man. Rumor had it she was related to Confederate General Jeb Stuart (whose real name was James Ewell Brown Stuart), but no one had ever actually confirmed the rumor. She was a presence—a tall woman who wore long black dresses and pulled her hair back in a severe bun.

When Rebecca and Cheslee entered the University of Georgia at Athens on the same day in 1949, it was not by chance. Rebecca had discovered through her extensive grapevine that Cheslee was planning to attend the school, so, rather than go to Sweet Briar or Hollins in Virginia, where her best friend Millie was heading, she made her plans to stay in Athens and become a Georgia Bulldog.

On the first day of school, she made sure that she "bumped into" Cheslee, and that was that. Although the men and women were kept segregated by dormitories and by fraternities, they could keep company before curfew hours.

Cheslee studied engineering. Rebecca studied Cheslee, although, ostensibly, she was training to be a teacher. His grades soared, while hers were mediocre. She was more intelligent than her grades demonstrated.

At the end of their freshman year, Cheslee and Rebecca were walking along the perimeter of the campus, just before his last final exam. "Rebecca," he said, "I don't think your heart is in school. Is it?"

"No, Cheslee, it isn't," she replied. "My heart is in your heart."

He stopped walking. He took both of her hands in his and looked directly into her eyes. "What do you mean?" he asked. "What does a gorgeous woman like you see in someone like me?"

"I see a man in you, Cheslee," she answered. "And I simply love you. How can I love school when I love you more?"

He didn't know what else to say. He grabbed her and pulled her close to him, kissed her hard on her mouth and whispered, "I love you, too. I promise I'll make a life with you."

He was shaking; she was calm. She had achieved her goal; he had no idea what to do next.

His mother knew, though. "Well, honey, get that girl a ring and set a date for a wedding! We can have it right here, at Lindenwood," she said. "She will make you a fine wife. We will be happy together, right here."

The extravagant wedding took place just before school began, in August 1950. The society reporter for *The Atlanta Constitution* attended the affair, and wrote a detailed article for the newspaper. Four-hundred guests gathered to see the spectacle, sweating under the blazing Georgia sun, and only ten fainted, which surprised Cheslee's mother. She expected to have at least 25 fainters.

Even U.S. Senator Richard Russell, Jr., came down from Washington to attend the event.

But the stunning bride, wearing a 20-foot train made of imported satin accented by thousands of pearls and embroidered white roses, was the center of attention. Cheslee himself almost fainted as he saw her walking down the aisle on the arm of her father, to become his bride.

They were both 20 years old.

Cheslee went back to school and finished his degree in engineering, while Rebecca returned to Lindenwood, moving in with her mother-in-law, who arranged to have part of the house remodeled so that they could have some semblance of privacy. Maude brought in carpenters, plumbers, and electricians and made a lovely small kitchen and dining area, a bedroom with a small attached bathroom, a sitting area, and even a medium-sized living room with a screened-in porch off the back. It was a delightful living space for newlyweds, and Rebecca so appreciated these efforts.

Maude loved Rebecca—her breeding, her manners, her wit, her effervescent air. She could tell by looking at Rebecca when Cheslee passed that the younger woman adored her son. *This was indeed a match made in heaven,* Maude would think to herself, smiling silently as she watched the newlyweds lightly touch each other's hands or shoulders. *God answered my prayers, bringing a good southern girl for my Cheslee.*

Maude started to worry, however, when they did not become pregnant right away. In fact, it took nearly four years before she learned she would finally become a grandmother.

"Mother," Cheslee said, "we need to talk to you." He held Rebecca's hand, firmly, as she looked at the floor, with a slight grin on her face. She couldn't look at Maude directly, instead staring at her tiny feet.

Cheslee cleared his throat. He stammered and then finally found the words. "Mother, we are going to have a baby."

Maude cut him off. "When? Where? Here? A baby? Here, at Lindenwood? Oh, my, Cheslee! What wonderful news!"

Only then did Rebecca feel as if she could make eye contact with her mother-in-law. They looked at each other with fondness and admiration, then the tears began.

Of course, Cheslee wanted a boy, but Rebecca didn't care whether it was a boy or a girl. She knew that, with Cheslee as its father, the baby would be beautiful and strong, no matter what its gender would be. She knew the Prescott genes were strong, and that her own background consisted of ancestors who had overcome many generations of adversity.

She could hardly wait to meet this baby.

CHAPTER 5

March 1954

On March 19, at four in the morning, Rebecca, who had not been sleeping, got out of bed and moved into the living room. She began to walk around in circles.

Cheslee stirred a little but didn't rise until his usual time of six AM.

"Rebecca, are you all right?" he asked, rubbing his eyes.

"No. No, I am not," she said, with a distinct edge in her voice. "Leave me alone."

"I can't leave you alone," he replied. "Are you going into labor, honey?"

"I don't know. I've never been in labor before. How would I know? Leave me alone!"

He moved behind her as she continued walking in circles and gently put his hands on her shoulders.

"I think we should call the doctor," he said, trying to remain calm.

"What can *he* do? He's a jerk!" she said.

Cheslee had never heard Rebecca talk that way before. She was in another world, it seemed.

Maude was already awake. She grabbed her robe from the bed stead and ran out of the bedroom.

"We are calling the doctor—aren't we, Cheslee?" Maude said, trying to reassure her.

She looked at her son, who was frozen in his steps. "Aren't we, Cheslee?"

"Oh, yes, yes," he replied, dialing the number as quickly as his shaking hands could.

Waiting at the front door of Athens Community Hospital with a wheel-chair was Miss Hilda Baxter, RN, one of Dr. Blevins's maternity nurses.

"Hello, honey, let's go!" she said to Rebecca, putting her in the chair. "The race is on!"

Cheslee parked, then went to the front desk. No receptionist was there—it was too early in the morning—so he made his way up to the maternity ward by following the signs. He was stopped by a huge sign: "FATHERS WAITING AREA"—with an arrow pointing to the right.

What? I'm not allowed? What am I supposed to do now? Just sit and stew?

He went to the waiting room and found one other father sitting, reading an outdated issue of *Look* magazine. The other man said, "Is this your first?"

"Yes," replied Cheslee. "And you?"

"Fourth," said the man, who didn't even look up from the magazine. "You get used to it."

"Oh," said Cheslee. "You do?"

"Yeah," the man said. "I'm just hoping this time it's a boy. We have three girls at home."

Soon after, Dr. Blevins appeared at the door.

"Mr. Prescott?" he said.

Cheslee jumped up, as if awakening from a dream. "Yes?"

"Mr. Prescott, this baby is in a breech position. We tried to move the baby so that the head would be positioned properly, but this is a stubborn one. We need to do a Cesarean section," the doctor explained. "This means that we will need to do major surgery and will have to completely anesthetize your wife. You understand. I will send the nurse out so that you can sign the necessary authorizations. We will have a baby in no time."

Cheslee froze. Now what?

"Oh…oh, yes, doctor, whatever you say is best. Can you just tell her I love her and that I am sorry?"

"Sorry? For what? You didn't create this situation, Mr. Prescott," the doctor assured him. "These things just happen. There's no blame to assign. I'll be back soon."

And the doctor disappeared behind two swinging doors that stayed in motion for what seemed like an eternity to Cheslee.

Tick, tock, tick, tock, tick, tock.

Tick, tock, tick, tock, tick, tock.

Finally, Dr. Blevins appeared again, this time with a smile on his face, his surgical mask hanging down from one ear.

"Mr. Prescott, you have a beautiful baby boy, and your wife did very well. She'll be asking for you once the anesthesia wears off. But if you want to see your boy, I can take you to the nursery."

Cheslee jumped up.

"Yes, yes, I want to see my boy! Thank you, Dr. Blevins! Thank you, thank you, thank you!" And off they went through the swinging doors.

Without looking up, the still-waiting father sighed, "HE got MY boy."

CHAPTER 6

The First Day

My father was disappointed that his first two children had been girls—my sisters Debbie and Donna—so when the doctor came out and told my father that I was born, he was ecstatic that he finally got his boy. He could teach me everything he knew about baseball. Almost from the time I could grab anything, my dad gave me a ball.

And now, in Jamestown, New York, in Single-A baseball. I'm surrounded by guys whose dads, mothers or coaches also worked with them all *their* lives. Most of them were drafted in rounds higher than I was. They probably got bigger signing bonuses, too. They were stars of their high school or college teams. They were all-stars on traveling teams or were picked by *Parade* magazine to be on All-America teams.

I was an all-star, too. I was all-New England pitcher of the year in 1972, when I was a senior in high school.

But here, no one can rest on his laurels. We're all starting from scratch.

At first day of practice, the pitchers are on one side of this field, which seems, from where I stand, to be as big as Fenway Park. The fielders and catchers are on the other side.

Cesar brings us together in a huddle. He grimaces as he focuses on speaking in English. What comes out, though, remains *Spanglish*—some English, some Spanish.

"*Hijos*," he begins, "*Béisbol* is serious business. *Chew* want to learn, *chew* need to listen. *Chew* think *chew* know everything about this game? *Chew* know nothing! *Nada!* I was once where *chew* are today. I thought I was the king of *béisbol* when I was 18 *jears* old! Ha! *Chew* listen, *chew* learn! *Chew* think *chew* the king, *chew* go home now. Go home to *chore* mama. She will say, 'Oh, my *leetle* king of *béisbol,* thank *chew* for coming home! I will cook for *chew*!' *Chore* mama is not here now. *Chew* are not the king anymore. *No hay los reyes en este equipe.* I have no kings on this team. If *chew* work hard, *chew* might become a duke or an earl, but no kings. *Entiende*? Understand?"

What? Of course, we're kings—kings of the hill of our hometowns, our college teams. This other part, this was new.

"Yes, sir," Bud says, in true southern gentleman-style.

A few other heads nod. I don't. I'm still processing; wondering if I'll be able to stand living in this podunk town. I'm still trying to figure out if my cleats even fit. Montreal Expos farm team? Do I have to learn French if I make it to the bigs?

"*Chew!*" Cesar yells at me. "Did *chew* even hear one word I said?"

"Yeah," I respond, "yeah, I did. No kings. Maybe dukes or earls. We need to listen."

"Oh, and I thought *chew* were taking a nap, *mi amigo* from Bos-tone," he says.

"Okay, let's get to work. *Chew!*" he pointed at Bud. "Mee-ster Southern Boy. *Chew* get on the mound for a minute."

He strolls to the other side of the field.

"What d'ya think he's gonna do?" I ask Bud.

"Probably get a catcher and then ask each one of us to throw," he says. "That's my guess."

Meanwhile, #15—Bobby Mangino—is looking me over. He's from New York, and Yankee lovers always hate Red Sox fans. It's a two-way street. We despise them back. It works out well for both sides that way.

Cesar returns with #22, a short, stocky guy wearing his catcher's mask on the back of his head, fooling with the straps on his chest protector. He's got no idea if any of us can actually aim a ball with accuracy, or if we'll be wild in the streets.

"This is Russ," says Cesar. "He going behind the plate. *Chew* throw to him. I tell *chew* what to throw. Simple?"

"Okay," Bud agrees, and he sets his foot on the rubber strip on the mound. I can see his hand shake a little—pressure from being first, I guess, but his face looks confident. Dad would like him.

Cesar has a basket of balls behind Bud. He hands one to Bud as Russ gets into the catcher's crouch.

"Toss a few, nice, easy, to warm up," Cesar says. "Nothing fast or breaking. Just toss."

Bud lobs a few to Russ and the balls are sent back. Easy. Just like playing catch in the backyard with Dad.

After about ten of those, Cesar stops Bud.

"Now, what *chew* got, Mee-ster South? What is *chore* best pitch? Fast ball? Curve? Sinker? Can *chew* throw a knuckleball?" He laughs at the idea.

Bud half smiles. "No, sir, I definitely cannot throw a knuckleball. Let's see."

Bud looks at Russ, as if searching for a sign during a real game, pulls his glove to his chest, secures his right foot on the pitching rubber, lifts his left leg at a ninety-degree angle, winds up his right arm, and, while landing on the left leg, throws a scorcher of a fastball into Russ's glove.

"Lookin' good!" Cesar says. "Throw a few more, then let me see *chore* curve ball."

Man, Bud looks great. I'm a little nervous. I hear Dad's voice.

"Jimmy, you're good. You're among the best. You need to build your confidence, but, wow, think of all I've taught you and what you can learn from good coaching. Everything's gonna work out fine."

"Okay, Dad," I mutter to myself. "*I just wish I believed it, now that I see* this *guy throw.*"

Bud throws a curve that breaks to the left. I wonder if it breaks to the right on left-handed hitters. We don't know, because we don't have any hitters. Yet.

Cesar puts a few more pitchers through the same paces. There is Alex Gibson (#24) from St. Louis, Missouri, Marion (yes, that's his name—named after John Wayne) McGhee (#37) from Missoula, Montana, Richie Newman (#14) from Whittier, California, Julio Nieves (#19) from Ciudad Juarez, Mexico, Jerry Malone (#33) from Natchez, Mississippi, and Mangino (#15).

Then he calls me. "Hey, Bos-tone boy! *Chew're* next!"

I adjust the glove on my left hand and walk to the mound. I play with the dirt on the mound a little with my cleats, a familiar part of my routine when I pitch.

"Hey, Bos-tone! We ain't got all day. Let's go!" Cesar says.

So I take my warm-up tosses with Russ. Smooth and easy. I imagine I'm five years old, tossing with Dad.

"Warm-up's done!" Cesar announces. "Show me what *chew* got, Bos-tone."

Get your bearings, I tell myself. Don't be wild. Just pitch. Just throw. Don't be an idiot. Focus. That's what dad would say.

I stand on the mound, one foot balanced, the other one cocked, the way a horse does when he's at rest. Then I put my right foot on the rubber, lean down at the waist as if looking for a sign from Russ, stand up straight, look to my left as if there were a runner on base. I hear a laugh from the other pitchers because of this. I take the ball in my right hand, rock back a little on the rubber, lift my left leg about three-and-a-half feet off the ground, cock my right hand back, fire off a fast ball, and land on my left foot, following through with my right hand.

The ball goes over Russ's head.

Cesar chuckles. "Try again," he says.

My next pitch is much better, fast and more accurate. It isn't in the imaginary strike zone, but it's close. After three more pitches, I'm throwing fast ball strikes.

"Okay, Bos-tone, *chew* got a curve ball?" Cesar asks.

I nod. I go through the same motions, but my curve ball doesn't break. It does sink, though.

"*Chew* call that a curve ball?" Cesar asks. "That look like a sinker ball from here."

I throw again, and this time it breaks, but it isn't in the strike zone. This is the same pattern as with my fastball. I don't know what's happening. I'm losing it. It takes me five pitches before I can throw a curveball strike. After that, Cesar moves on to the next pitcher, Andy McManus from Skowhegan, Maine (#12).

What the hell is wrong with me? I've been pitching in front of people since I was six years old! Is this the way it's going to be?

After the entire pitching staff has been tested, Cesar says, "Great work, everyone! *Chew* all look good. Teachable. Now I can think of what to fix. Homework. *Chew* all need homework!"

He lets out a huge belly laugh and walks away.

"Well, what did you think?" I ask Bud.

"Everyone was pretty nervous," he replies. "This isn't an easy thing to do, especially in front of all the people you're looking to beat out and move up to the next level."

"You looked really good," I say. "You didn't look like you were bothered by anything. How come?"

"Oh, that was because he had me go first," he answers. "That's always the easiest—get it over first. Then you can sit down and no one sees you sweat. You did fine, too, but you may have overthought the situation."

Overthought? Is that what I did?

"Do you think that's what happened?" I ask Bud.

"Yeah," he says, "I see it happen all the time. Don't worry, you'll be fine."

He puts his arm around my shoulder and drapes it over the team name on my uniform.

"Come on," he says, "let's get off this field and check out the rest of this place. We're going to be spending a lot of time here."

In the distance I catch a glimpse of Mangino, standing by himself. Mangino's refusing to socialize or talk.

Bud and I walk across the grass. He still has his arm across my shoulders. Bud seems to have no inhibitions, no issues with people who come from different backgrounds or have varying preferences.

He could be a politician.

CHAPTER 7

A Baseball High

I find out Bud and I were born one day—and worlds—apart.

He tells me he has no brothers or sisters, and I say, "My two sisters would throw you for a loop. They're something else."

"What do you mean?" he asks.

"Well, Debbie—she's the oldest, looks just like my mother. She's also wicked smart, and I think she'll be rich someday, based on her brains," I explain. "She's always been at the top of her class. And she's six feet tall."

"Six feet tall? Wow." Bud says.

"My other sister, Donna, isn't as outgoing as Debbie."

"Is she six feet tall, too?"

"Naw, she's only five-foot-ten," I answer. "At least I'm taller than either one of them—the 'baby' brother."

"My grandmother says that after my mother had a problem giving birth to me, she decided she wouldn't have any more children," Bud explains. "It's too bad. We have a really big ole house. It even has a name—Linden-wood—and it could have used a few more kids running around."

"No one names bungalows like the ones in Weymouth," I say.

We both laugh.

"Hey, what's up with Mangino?" he asks. "Why won't he even sit with us in the locker room?"

"I dunno," I say. "He just seems to want to keep to himself. He comes from New York City, you know. People there are kinda like that, I think."

We get up, walk away, and go back out on the field. "Smell that grass," he says. "Take that smell in, all the way in, and just enjoy it. There's no better perfume in the world than the aroma of a baseball field."

He's right. There's nothing better than the smell that fills every corner, every inch, of a ballpark on a sunny spring day, right after it's been mowed almost down to the quick, right after the foul lines have been repainted and the pitcher's mound has been repacked with new dirt and watered.

The aroma makes me feel high. I bet it's like sniffing cocaine or drinking too much tequila.

But I've never done that. I've only gotten high on baseball.

CHAPTER 8

Paul Anderson

I return to 1048 Maryland Avenue. Mrs. Anderson is cooking up a storm in the kitchen, humming a cheery tune. Her meatloaf smells so good, it almost wipes out the lingering smells of the ballpark.

Mr. Anderson is parked in his favorite recliner. He's instructed me never, ever to sit in it.

"Instant death if you sit in my chair. And you know how I will know?" he asked. "My butt cheeks have sculpted a place for me in this chair, and they know by instinct if anyone else sits in it. There's no Goldilocks and the three bears here. It's all done by butt cheeks."

Tonight he says, "I see your name in the paper, kid. You're on the roster. Good thing. We don't have to send you home—yet."

Yet? What does he mean by that? Have they had other ballplayers sent home after just the first day? What the hell? I have no intention of leaving after one day. I haven't even pitched to a single batter.

"Dad, cut it out," Paul says. "He just got here. Give him a chance."

I sigh.

On this team, everyone was a standout, and we're all competing for the same thing: to get to The Show. We don't care if it's The Expos, The Senators, The Braves, The Tigers. It's whatever team thinks we're good enough to play in the majors.

At dinner, there's very little talk. We're too engrossed in eating meatloaf, mashed potatoes, gravy, green beans, Pillsbury pop-up rolls, and butter. Paul drinks Pepsi-Cola. I have milk. Mr. Anderson has a Pabst Blue Ribbon beer. Mrs. Anderson drinks a cup of coffee, which I can smell from across the table.

"So, Jimmy," Mrs. Anderson says, "how was today at the ballpark? Did you have fun?"

"Well, I wouldn't exactly call it 'fun,'" I respond. "I had to throw from the mound in front of the pitching coach, and I was kinda nervous."

"How'd the other guys do?" Mr. Anderson asks.

"One of them—the first one to pitch—was terrific," I reply. "The rest were kinda like me, only not so wild from the get-go. I was kinda wild on my first few pitches."

"Oh, you're probably being too hard on yourself," Mrs. Anderson says.

"No, I *was* wild, but I did settle down," I assure them. "The pitching coach is from the Dominican Republic. He calls me 'Bos-tone boy.'"

They chuckled.

"Where are the rest of the people from?" Paul asks.

"They're from all over the country, and a few from outside the U.S.," I tell him. "I met one pitcher from Puerto Rico, but that's actually a U.S. territory."

"It is?" Mr. Anderson says. "That's surprising. I saw 'West Side Story' at the Jamestown Theatre, and that's not what I would think."

"Dad, what a dopey thing to say!" Paul says. "That's a stupid musical, not a historical play!"

Mr. Anderson glares at Paul.

"'I like to be in America, okay by me in America, for a small fee in America'—that's what they say in the song, Paul, when they say everyone from Puerto Rico wants to come here. So how could it be part of the U.S.?"

"Guys from Puerto Rico fight in Vietnam!" Paul says. They get drafted. Does that make you feel any better?"

Paul slams his fork on the table, and heads for his room.

"Sheesh! What's wrong with him?" Mr. Anderson asks.

"I'm just remembering what I saw at the Jamestown Theatre. It was a good play, I thought. Lots of dancing and singing. Kept me awake. Not like that long-hair Shakespeare stuff *she* likes to see," he waves his fork at Mrs. Anderson.

"You need culture in your life, Bill," she says, "and it's my job to make sure you get it."

"Culture, scmulture," he mutters, picking up a newspaper and folding it back, making loud, rustling noises in the process. "I'd rather watch TV in my comfy chair."

I decide I should excuse myself. As I walk up the oak stairs, covered with faux oriental rug treads, I hear music coming from Paul's room, and I smell something, too. Incense. My sister Debbie burns that in her room at home. It's big on college campuses, she says.

"If my words could talk...ripple, in still waters..."

I recognize The Grateful Dead. Debbie likes them, too. She wanted to go to Woodstock, but Dad wouldn't let her.

I knock on Paul's door. "Paul? It's me, Jimmy. Can I come in?"

I hear rustling, the sound of a needle moving on the vinyl record, and the music stops.

"Yeah, Jimmy, come on in. It's a mess in here, though."

I open the door. Piles of clothes are everywhere—jeans, sweat pants, t-shirts, socks—and I presume they're dirty, but all you can smell is incense. His record player looks like a blue suitcase.

Album jackets are scattered all over the place. The Grateful Dead. Jimi Hendrix. The Beatles. Big Brother and the Holding Company, with Janis Joplin. The Doors. Pearls Before Swine. Crosby, Stills and Nash. He doesn't seem to take care of the records themselves.

"Hey, if you can find a spot, sit down," he says, trying to be a good host. "Yeah, yeah, I know, I'm not much of a housekeeper. My mom just shuts the door and groans whenever she looks in. Maybe I don't want her in here, you know?"

Thinking about the sparseness of my room across the hall, I say, "Yeah, I know. You've got your own life to live, and your own secrets."

"Yeah, you've got it," he replies. "Secrets. I've got a lot of them. Hey, you ever smoke anything?"

"Anything?" I ask. "What do you mean, 'anything'?"

"You know, 'anything,' like grass, hash, anything like that," he says.

"No way!" I tell him. "I'm in training. I need to stay away from that stuff. I'm trying to make the major leagues."

"Oh—okay, no problem," he says, stepping back from me as far as he can, given the mound of stuff behind him. "I was just asking. The last guy who lived here was kinda into this stuff."

"The last guy? Really? Was he a ballplayer, too?"

"Yeah. He's still on the team. They didn't promote him to AA this year."

"You don't mean..."

"Bobby Mangino? Yeah. He lived here last year. He and I got high together all the time. My mom never knew, or if she did, she never said anything. He's a New York City boy. He's into all that stuff."

"My sister Debbie does that stuff," I say, "but she's a college girl. All those people are into that. And drinking, too."

"So you don't drink, either?" he asks.

"Nah," I reply. "I never got into that stuff, either. I was too busy playing ball."

"Huh...A teetotaler who plays baseball. That's a switch," he says. Most of the time, we get people who are accomplished drinkers, at least. We'll see how that is by the end of the season."

"I'm in training," I emphasize, again. "I need to stay in shape."

"Sure, Jimmy. Sure."

Paul puts on a new record.

"Truckin'...Got my chips cashed in...Keep truckin'..."

It's my cue to leave.

I go across the hall to my room and kick off my shoes, but I don't get undressed. I lie on my bed with my ball cap on my head, staring at the ceiling.

Is this what you were talking about, Dad? I thought you were talking about the things I'd have to worry about when the coach put a ball in my hand, not this stuff.

And in my head I hear Crosby, Stills and Nash: *"You...who are on the road...must have a code...that you can live by...teach your children well..."*

You taught me how to throw a ball, bat, field, endure the heat, the cold, and read the way an umpire calls balls and strikes. But this?

Across the hall, in his room, Paul is settling in. His room was filled with incense and patchouli. The music gets a little louder. I hear Mr. Anderson in the living room turn the TV up louder. It's a duel.

CHAPTER 9

Silence

I stumble down the thick oak stairs at the Anderson house the next morning.

The railing swirls at the end in big concentric wooden circles that look just like how my head feels—churning, turning, unable to stop moving.

I couldn't sleep last night, overthinking this whole thing. I'm a good pitcher, dammit, and I can do this. My dad wouldn't have brought me here if he didn't believe in me. I wouldn't have come here if I didn't believe in myself. Right?

I sit down at the breakfast table. Paul isn't there. Mrs. Anderson seems worried about me.

"Honey, are you okay?" she asks.

"I didn't sleep too well last night," I reply.

"The sound wars between my husband and Paul got to you, I guess," she says.

"That was part of it," I answer, "but also, today I have to work out and also pitch to my teammates from the mound. I was overthinking it pretty much all night, I think."

"First day jitters, I guess, and your dad's not here to support you," she says. "It's really normal. You're not all that far off, you know. You're not the first ballplayer we've had living here, and I hope you won't be the last. You come from a nice family, and I think you're a nice boy."

A nice boy. Yup. That's me. A teetotaling baseball player from the South Shore of Boston. A goody-two shoes, or so says your son.

"I'm trying to stay focused," I reply. "I get pretty worked up sometimes."

"You'll be fine. Here, have some orange juice and eggs. I have bacon, too. You like bacon? Sausage? And I made blueberry muffins! I don't have those very often. If you want, you can take a couple of them with you to the ballpark."

"Thanks so much, Mrs. Anderson," I say.

I eat breakfast, trying to chew slowly and enjoy the food, but my mind is still racing. I lose count of how many strips of bacon I shove down my throat.

"You're a good eater!" Mrs. Anderson exclaims. "You'll need all that energy today. You're right, it's a big day."

A big day. A big day. One side of my brain says, "What did you expect?" The other side screams, "Who cares? You're a star! You're up for this challenge!"

My interior self-argument is interrupted by the sound of a horn outside from the car pool taking me to the park. I grab a third muffin, pick up my duffel bag, and run out to the car.

"Get in, Bailey, we're late!" the driver commands.

The other guys won't move over, so I weasel my way into the middle back seat.

To my left is Jamie Kirk, an outfielder from Houston, and to my right, Joey Tidwell, a second baseman from Gainesville, Florida.

We're all in the same boat: all-stars in our high schools, Babe Ruth and Connie Mack ball. People at home knew who we are. Here, we are essentially nothing but three passengers jammed into the back seat of a Dodge station wagon—until we can prove otherwise.

CHAPTER 10

Athens Buries a Daughter
of the Confederacy

Bud's grandmother's death surprised him, but it wasn't a surprise. Maude Elwell Prescott was 86 years old, but Bud thought she'd live forever. She was his rock, the one he went to when he had things to say his mother and father wouldn't understand.

For her part, Maude doted on Bud even more than most grandmothers did on their offspring's offspring. Bud was her one and only, and Maude was a wealthy woman who made sure he had everything he needed–and then some.

Bud never disappointed his grandmother. He wasn't distracted by the many girls who threw themselves at him; he knew what he wanted, and he knew how to get it. He was playing this summer in Jamestown, but he was going to Vanderbilt in the fall. He would be majoring in biology, because, as his grandmother always said, "What if this baseball thing doesn't work out? What would you want to be?"

"A doctor," he would respond, without hesitation. "I would want to work with athletes."

"So an orthopedist?" she would ask.

"Yes."

He missed those talks already.

They discussed everything: from the news of the day to economics, how to treat women and expect to be treated in return, how to drive a car, how to manage money, and how to stay cool in the oppressive Georgia heat.

He was intrigued by her thoughts on race.

Her own parents had owned and lived with slaves, and her grandparents had been slave traders. She herself never believed that people should be owned and made into slaves, and yet, she couldn't deny that slave holders were part of her own ancestry. She also didn't understand why people were so resistant to allowing free blacks to vote, or why people couldn't live with the idea that black people were equal to whites.

"We need to give them some time to grow out of their prejudices," she would tell Bud. "Maybe with time, they will change. We are all God's children, no matter what color our skin is."

Bud picked up on that. He often stepped in when racial tensions arose at his high school. If someone tried to single out a person of color based simply on race, Bud would often step into the argument to diffuse the situation. He endured lots of epithets flung his way by some of the "good ole boys," but he didn't care.

Now he looked up to see his father waving to him. Bud grabbed his hastily-packed duffel bag and ran over to him.

"Thanks for picking me up, Daddy. How are you holding up?"

"Fair to middling, I guess," Cheslee replied.

Bud could see tears welling up in his father's eyes. Then he felt the hot, stinging liquid coming from his own eyes as the salty stream ran down his cheeks. His face was flushed, his nose started running. No handkerchief or tissue in sight.

I am a blithering idiot, he thought. *My grandmother would not want to see me this way, even after she died. She would want me to hold my head up high and move on. But to see dad like this...he's trying to be brave. Maybe we shouldn't be brave. Just this once.*

His father wasn't the hugging type, but Bud didn't care. He put his arms around his daddy and drew him close to his chest. Cheslee began to sob into his son's shirt. He clutched on to Bud's back and shoulder blades, trying to regain his composure, but it wasn't working. People walking by them were staring, but neither of them cared. Bud gently touched the top of his head. "It's okay, Daddy. It's okay."

"I'm 'bout cried out, son," Cheslee said. "I know she was old and all, and I know she had a good life, but what am I goin' to do without her? She was so good to me, to all of us. She loved you, your mother, too. She wadn't one of those mothers-in-law who didn't like the woman her son married. She adored your mother from day one.

"And she was so strong. My daddy died before I knew I had a daddy, and she carried on. What can you say about someone like her?"

"I don't know, Daddy," Bud said. "We all are richer for her being with us, and poorer now that she's gone. I don't mean money rich and poor, I mean our lives. Oh, hell, I don't know what I mean. I mean that I'm not sure I can face Lindenwood without her in it. I will be looking around the corners for her, expecting to hear her voice, see her face. I was hoping she would come see me pitch some time. And see me graduate from Vanderbilt."

"She was looking forward to that," Cheslee commented, nodding his head. "She talked about it often. But I guess her heart just gave out. She just didn't wake up. She died peaceful-like. Guess that's the best way to go. She knew we loved her. I'm sure of it."

"Yes, Daddy, she knew," Bud replied, "but what a big hole this leaves in our lives." And he put his hand on his father's shoulder as they walked out together toward the family car, on their way home to Lindenwood.

Everyone who was *anyone* in Athens or Atlanta came to the funeral. Even Governor Jimmy Carter and his wife Roslyn came to pay their respects. They came in a private car, not a huge limousine, although they did have state police protection. They sat in the front pew at the First Baptist Church, next to Cheslee, Rebecca and Bud.

Bud looked over at his grandmother's oak casket, standing in the middle of the aisle. One half was draped with the state flag of Georgia, while the other half was covered in white lace. He noticed the gold handles and the intricate carving along the sides, thinking that his grandmother, this exceptional woman, deserved to end her life in luxury, by having her body find its eternal rest in such an ornate specimen of craftsmanship.

The pastor spoke for quite a while about the many things that Maude Ewell Prescott had done for the community, and how, when women didn't have the vote, she was one of the most outspoken southern women who fought for women to have the right to enter the voting booth, just like men. Much to the chagrin of some of her neighbors, she had also allowed a group of civil rights workers from the north to use part of Lindenwood as a classroom, as they sought to teach black residents to read and write as part of a voter registration drive in the 1960s. She'd had to fend off a few visits from the Ku Klux Klan about that. She had confronted them, all alone, on the front lawn of Lindenwood, roaring at them to go home, calling them out by identifying them by their voices.

"You can't fool me behind those white hoods!" she yelled. "I know who each and every one of you is! I helped some of your families when you were in need, and this is how you thank me? And if you light that cross on my lawn, or set my house on fire, you might as well kill me, too. Kill everything you see here, but you won't kill my spirit. You think you stand for 'the old south?' You're nothing but a bunch of hoodlums!"

And they went away. They came back a couple of times, acting tough again, but she scoffed at them gave them the same lecture. Each time, she shamed them into going home without completing their mission, or without interfering in hers, often by threatening to call their mothers or grandmothers to report their rude behavior.

At the funeral, several others followed and made statements about "Miss Maude" and her contributions to society—how she always had a kind word and would help anyone she knew about who needed financial or moral assistance.

Bud's mind wandered throughout the talking. He couldn't focus. He heard a few words here and there, but he just kept thinking about the fact that he would go back to Lindenwood tonight and would be looking for her and she wouldn't be there. She'd never see him graduate from Vanderbilt. Never know if he ever made the major leagues. Never know if he had children of his own.

Then, slowly, Cheslee made his way to the pulpit—another ornate carved oak masterpiece, this time with a spiral staircase leading up to the top. It stood about four feet higher than the floor where the altar was located, and had been the scene of many a fire-and-brimstone sermon in its day.

But not today. Today Cheslee at first simply thanked people for coming to help say good-bye to a wonderful woman.

Then he began:

"I know that everyone you meet will tell you that their mothers are one of a kind, that they have overcome all sorts of obstacles, and that they have inspired so many people. I can say the same thing about my mother, only more so.

"Everyone can look at our house and say, 'Oh, those rich folk who live behind those white columns! They must have so much money, they don't know what to do with it!' Well, Momma knew what to do with it, and she helped so many people, so many times. After my daddy died, she vowed that she would help other people whose families had no daddies to help them. She would go to the hospitals and look for new mothers who had been abandoned and try to get them on track. She didn't care what they looked like, what color they were, what religion they followed. She always told me that they were human beings, and that was what was important."

He paused, reached into his pocket for a balled-up handkerchief, and dabbed at his eyes.

"You are all human beings," he continued. "And your presence here today demonstrates to the world that there is hope. I look out at this congregation, and I see such an amazing representation of people from all walks of life. I see the famous people who have their pictures in the newspaper. I see people from all races and creeds. I see young and old, rich and not-so-rich. But what I don't see, thanks to what my mother taught me, is any *ordinary* people. Every one of you is extraordinary. Live every day like it is an exquisite work of art. That's what my mother did. That is what she would want you to do.

"Again, I thank you for taking time out of your busy schedules to come here today. We are so grateful as a family that you are here. You are today—and always will be—part of our family."

He bowed his head, looked over at the casket, put the handkerchief in his pocket, turned his back and started down the steps, holding on to the railing to ensure that he didn't stumble and fall. By that time, he was noticeably crying, but he was also thankful that he had been able to get through speaking in front of the large crowd.

Cheslee went to the front row, shook hands with Governor and Mrs. Carter, then took Rebecca's hand. She was already holding onto Bud. The three of them walked hand-in-hand to the back of the church, nodding along the way to people they knew or thought they knew. Of course, everyone knew them; they were pillars of this community, in the same way that the columns held up the enormous front porch at Lindenwood.

After mindlessly shaking a few hands, Cheslee escorted Rebecca and Bud to a waiting limousine.

The three Prescotts got into the cavernous vehicle with burnt-sienna leather seats and boxes of tissues tucked into every possible nook. Bud noticed how the leather squeaked when he moved back and forth, just like his glove did when he worked the ball back and forth as he was deciding which pitch to throw in a given situation. He began playing with the leather with his pitching hand, working it like he would if he had a new glove that needed to be broken in.

Bud could hear the click of the directional signal as the limo pulled away from the church. They were leading a long line of cars to the Oconee Hill Cemetery, near the University of Georgia, where Maude's body would join that of her long-gone husband in the family plot.

The procession was so long that they had to hire an additional ten off-duty police officers to handle the traffic. The cemetery itself would have a problem accommodating all of these people, so some would have to leave their cars and walk to the burial site.

Bud felt as if they were driving in molasses. Around this corner. Around that corner. Up this hill. Take a left. Take a right. His head was spinning again.

Finally, Bud saw a granite arch with "Oconee Hill" carved into the top. He kept playing with the leather seats, rubbing his pitching hand in a circular motion, back and forth, forth and back.

The limo stopped in front of an enormous bleached granite stone, about eight feet wide by about six feet tall. In large bas relief letters, the name PRESCOTT was visible and could probably be read from half a mile away. He saw his grandfather's name: Chester Lee Prescott, born June 7, 1884, died February 16, 1937, with a Veterans' emblem around the carved stone.

My dad's name is a combination of his father's two names, he thought. *Chester and Lee. I wonder why I hadn't realized that before.*

Then, next to his name, the newly carved letters of his grandmother's name brought him back to reality: Maude Ewell Prescott, born October 6, 1884, died June 10, 1972. He could see where the stone mason had left rough-hewn marks in the granite. He was sure that Rebecca and Cheslee would want him to come back later and make it smoother.

Surrounding the stone were thousands of flowers. Different colors of roses. Poppies. Hydrangeas. Baby's breath. Tulips, even though they were out of season. Calla lilies. Snapdragons. And so many different kinds of ferns to accentuate the stunning arrangements.

My grandmother would have preferred that people spent their money on people who don't have enough food to eat. She always quoted that old Carter Family song about "Give me the roses while I live." There must be thousands of dollars in flowers here–blossoms that will wither with time, but Grandma would say that if you feed people's bellies, they will grow strong, and she would have scolded people for spending money on flowers when there were so many hungry mouths to feed.

On the other side of the stone was a huge, deep hole for the casket. He walked around and looked down into the dirt, which had been cleared away to accommodate the great oak box that contained his grandmother's remains.

How can I leave her here, alone and in the cold? How can I just go back to playing baseball, when I know she's alone here?

The tears came again, hot and wet down his cheeks. Where was his handkerchief? He left it in the limo. He ran back and dug it out of the back seat, rubbing the leather one more time for comfort.

People began to gather near the gravesite. The pastor, with his long robes and colorful scarf around his neck, held his Bible open. He waited for people to gather in a semi-circle around the gravesite before he began to speak.

"Thank you for coming, as we say goodbye to our dear Maude," said the pastor. "This is never easy, and it's especially not easy when we have a woman like her, who has been a pillar of this community for so many years. We have been so fortunate here in this little corner of Georgia to have had our own Georgia peach..."

A cry came out from the back of the crowd, so he had to pause. Someone was loudly, uncontrollably sobbing and needed to be consoled.

"...our own Georgia peach, who loved not only her family, all of whom she cherished, but also her extended family–all of you here, and many who could not come today–as well as her home state of Georgia and the entire United States of America. She was a true patriot and a proud daughter of this land. She fought for women to get the vote and showed enormous dignity when she walked up the stairs of the court house for the first time to register so that she could cast her first vote. She showed many of us the way, on so many issues, in so many turbulent times.

"Let us pray...

"On behalf of her only son, Cheslee, his lovely wife, Rebecca, and their son—the grandson whom she cherished, Cameron—she called him 'Bud'—I thank you once again for supporting them through this difficult time."

A large winch lifted the coffin high above the hole and slowly, slowly placed the casket into the opening. The pastor motioned to each of the family members to take a handful of dirt and throw it on top of the coffin. Cheslee went first, then Rebecca, then Bud, who threw the dirt as if it were a fastball, slamming the grains against the oak.

Then Rebecca went over to the flowers, found the reddest rose she could, plucked it out from the arrangement, and tossed it on top of the dirt.

"Rest in peace, my friend," she said, "for you were truly my friend, not just my mother-in-law, the mother of my love. I would have never made it to this day without you." She lowered her head. Cheslee put his arm around her and walked her back to the limo.

Bud stayed at the gravesite for a few minutes longer.

"Bud," said a small voice from behind him, "I'm so sorry that you lost your grandmother. I wish I had something good to say, but I can only say I'm sorry."

He turned quickly and saw Jenny Murphy, one of the girls who had chased him when they were in high school. She was wearing a navy blue dress accented by white pearls, a pearl bracelet and white shoes. Her brown-blonde hair was pulled back into a bun.

"Thank you, Jenny," he replied. "That means a lot to me. Where is your car? I'll walk you back to it."

"Oh, it's no bother," she said. "My brother Steve is with me. He can walk me back."

"No, I want to…If…If…If that's okay with you."

"Sure," she said. "Let's go. We had to park pretty far away."

CHAPTER 11

Bud's Back

Without Bud here, no one seems to talk much. Bud's the guy who gets everyone talking.

I strike up a conversation with a guy from upstate New York; Tim Jakubowski, He's from Troy, a factory town on the Hudson River.

"I went to Catholic Central High School," he says. "Yeah, we had nuns for teachers. They didn't hit me on the knuckles because I played ball. They treated the ballplayers pretty good because we won the Catholic school state championship."

"Any other guys from your school get drafted?" I ask.

"Yeah, a pitcher—Dougie Lannon. He's a lefty—not a bad thrower," he said. "A little late-breaking curve ball, but his fastball looks great. His dad is worried he's going to hurt his arm if he doesn't get good coaching, though."

"Who took him?"

"The Braves. They got some good coaches. They got them two Niekro brothers who throw knucklers, too."

He starts pounding on his glove and blowing Double Bubble gum bubbles, bigger than his face. One of them pops up into his ball cap, all over his eyes and nose, and he starts to laugh.

"And how about you?" he asks. "Where you from?"

I tell him about Weymouth, my dad and The Filly, and how he taught me all he knew about baseball, and how he gave up playing to stay with my mother.

"Shoot, ain't that stupid? I mean, I would never give up playing ball for some woman," he says.

"You never know what you'll do for love," I say. "But personally, I've never been in love, so I guess I don't know."

49

"Me, neither," he says. "Guess we'll find out some day."

"Yup."

"Oh, *girls*!" Skip yells, speaking to us. "It's time to stop the gossip and get to work! Bailey, get with Dominguez! Jakubowski—you're with Mick! Chop, chop!"

"Guess we got our orders," I say.

"Yup."

And off we go.

Four days later, Bud saunters into the locker room as everyone's getting suited up for practice.

"Hey, man! Great to see you!" I say.

He reaches out his hand to shake mine, and, before I know it, he's hugging me. "Great to be back, Jimmy," he says, "but I gotta tell you, it was hard. I still can't believe she's gone."

"I don't know what to say. What can I say? What can I do?"

"Nothin', man, just let's get out and play some ball," he says. "Give me some of that "Pahk the cahr in Hahvahd yahd talk!"

"You bet! Let me see how many 'rs' I can drop from words, so you can figure out how many lettahs I earned in high school!"

I catch a glimpse of Bobby Mangino, watching this whole scene. He should already be out on the field, running sprints or doing push-ups. He's a nosy jerk.

Bud and I walk onto the field together. Everyone starts to cheer Bud. Hoots and hollers go up to the sky and echo in the empty stadium.

Empty seats make a way different sound than a full stadium. They creak and rattle, and it makes my bones ache when no one is sitting in the seats. If it's raining and the seats are empty, that's one thing. But when the seats are empty on a day that the sun's shining, you have to wonder why people aren't coming to the game.

We're just practicing, but opening day is only ten days away. I scan the empty seats as the rest of the guys and the coaches come over to talk to Bud. He seems relieved to be back.

I'm relieved too. He has a calming influence on the team. He's the miracle glue.

Tomorrow we're going to have an on-field scrimmage with Geneva, an affiliate of the Washington Senators, whose home field is located in New York's Southern Tier.

I'm guessing Geneva is as much of a pit stop as Jamestown.

CHAPTER 12

Mangino

Bud had his foot up on a bench, lacing his cleats, when Bobby Mangino tapped his shoulder.

"Heard your grandmother died. Sorry."

"Thanks. It's Bobby, right?"

"Yeah. I ain't never known my grandmother, so I don't know what it's like to have one. What's it like?" he asked.

What's it like? She laughed at me when I was a rascal, even though she knew she should be scolding me. She was like the red clay Georgia soil, hard as a rock, until you dug into her soul. And she was like an angel sent from God for so many people—hungry, homeless, directionless people.

"My grandmother was quite a lady," Bud replied. "She was 86 years old and she lived a good life. She helped a lot of people in her time."

"Oh. Was she rich?"

"Well, I'd say she was quite comfortable," Bud said, "but she also gave a lot of her money away. My dad was her only child, and I was her only grandchild, so she kind of adopted a lot of the kids in the community, too."

"You live in a small town?" Bobby asked.

"Sort of. It's just outside Atlanta—Athens, Georgia," Bud replied. "It's where the University of Georgia is. We get to watch a lot of football. Georgia Bulldogs. And you?"

"Yonkers, New York," Bobby said, only he said "Yon-kahs."

"Near Yankee Stadium. My ma was livid when they didn't draft me."

"Ya know, I didn't care *who* drafted me, as long as *someone* did," Bud said.

"My ma has practically nothing, except for me and my little brother," Bobby said, then he stopped. He was telling this stranger too much.

"I bet she's a hard worker," Bud commented.

"Yeah, she works hard, but it seems she's got nothin' to show for it."

"She's got you," Bud said, "and here you are, playing baseball. That's something."

Yeah? The Yankees wouldn't even take me. What's to be proud of? Here I am in the podunk town, again, not even playing Double-A ball. Not even The Montreal Expos think I'm good enough to be promoted.

"Yeah, I guess," he replied. But the skin on his face felt like an oven being warmed up so a cake could bake.

"Anyways, I'm sorry you lost your grandmother."

"Thanks, man, I appreciate it," said Bud, reaching out to shake Bobby's hand.

Bobby didn't know how to respond, hesitated for a second, and finally shook Bud's hand.

It was one of the few times Bud would see Bobby smile.

CHAPTER 13

Meeting and Memory

"Listen up, guys," Skip says to the team gathered in the locker room. *I wish we had done this outside,* I think. *It smells so bad in here—all sweat and mold.*

"Now, we've got this scrimmage tomorrow. We're lucky to get a game-like scrimmage rather than play another intersquad. The team from Geneva's pretty good. They've got a couple of decent pitchers that Washington drafted. As you all know, the Senators aren't very good. They've had a few flashes in the pan, but they need a lot of help.

"Anyway, they have this Cuban hitter who escaped from Castro, and we need to be on the lookout for him. He's a hot hitter. Name's Valder—how do you say his name, Cesar?"

"Valderrama," Cesar replies, rolling the double "rs" in the way that only someone whose native language is Spanish can do, "related to a famous Cuban painter."

"Valderrama, Yulias Valderrama," Skip says, without rolling the double rs. "I don't know his whole story, but the buzz in this league is that he's the next Tony Oliva. So you pitchers—watch the signs when he comes up. Don't go rogue on me and decide what you're gonna throw. Pay attention to what your catcher calls for.

"They have a few other good players, I hear, but I'm not hearing much about their pitching. They're keeping that under wraps. We'll see tomorrow. So get a good night's sleep and be ready."

I couldn't wait to come up for air.

As I walk up the steps, my cleats tapping on the worn wooden stairs, the fragrance of newly-mown grass rescues me.

My memory creates more smells: hot dogs and beer, popcorn and cotton candy. I'm seven years old again, and Dad and I are waiting with our tickets in hand at the turnstiles on Lansdowne Street at Fenway Park, so we can watch batting practice.

The stands won't be empty for long.

CHAPTER 14

Internal Dialogue

I arrive at the field after my ride in the Dodge's back seat again, between Kirk and Tidwell, who, again, don't speak.

They walk well ahead of me, still not speaking to me or each other. Kirk is white and Tidwell is black, but I don't think that's it. It's 1972. Isn't all that stuff behind us? I mean, even the Yankees and the Red Sox are integrated.

But Jimmy, the devil on my shoulder says, *what if one of 'them' gets picked to go to the majors and you don't? Don't you think that's favoritism? I mean, they're getting a leg up on you because the government is trying to give them better opportunities, right?*

Not so! says the angel on the other shoulder *They're looking for the best ballplayers they can find. This is about winning, not about skin color.*

Yeah, you can believe that if you want to, the devil says. *But you should find some way to get an edge. You know, there are drugs...*

The angel pipes in. *This kid doesn't need your drugs. He's too good. His dad taught him everything he needs to know. Give it up!*

The two voices battle for a good ten minutes, about other things, too.

I'm confused. I never had problems making friends in Weymouth. I was the top dog. It was natural. But here I feel alone. And I don't have Debbie or Donna to ask for advice when I need it.

Paul Anderson wants me to relax, listen to some Grateful Dead, take a toke, burn some incense. Donna would say I should have a beer with the guys on the team to get to know them. And Debbie's usual advice is to go the Janis Joplin route and take a few sips of Southern Comfort, relax and enjoy where I am for a while.

Dad would say, *don't you dare blow this. Reflect on how hard you've worked to get here.*

But maybe it's Dad who worked hard to get here, not me.

Now that I'm here, maybe the next step is to find out how the world works outside baseball.

I've handled everything else up to now with no problem.

Maybe it's time I had a quick toke with Paul. Or developed a taste for beer, or whiskey.

I tell the angel and devil I've had enough.

TKO goes to the angel. For tonight.

CHAPTER 15

Creating a Line-Up

I walk down the dugout's rickety steps, through the hallway into the locker room. It's still pretty smelly from last night, but I detect a flowery odor from air freshener. Lilacs and roses.

The floral cover-up gets into my lungs, and I cough a little and sneeze a couple times.

I look behind me, and Mangino is there. For the first time since I've been here, he speaks to me.

"Whatsamatter, you been blowin' powder?"

"What?"

"Ah, come on! You know what I'm talkin' about! You been snortin' coke?"

"Absolutely not!" I replied. "I just can't stand the smell of the air freshener they sprayed in here."

"Oh, *that's* a good one! Now I've heard it all!" he snorted.

I could feel my eyes wrinkle and my mouth tighten. "I'm hiding nothin'! Besides, why do you get to know anything about me? I know nothin' about you!"

"All you need to know about me, Red Sox, is that the Yankees are better, and they're my team."

"I could give two shits about the Yankees. Billy Martin, Whitey Ford, Mickey Mantle? They don't give kids the time of day when they come to Fenway. Not impressed."

He comes charging after me, slamming me against a line of lockers. "Oh, so you're better than the Yankees?" he says.

"Get your hands off me, Mangino, or you'll find out more about me than you ever wanted to know."

Mick McDonald, the hitting coach, comes running over, and pushes us apart.

"Hey! What's goin' on here? Save it for the other team, okay?"

I try to shake his handprints off my shoulders.

"Who started this?" Mick asks. "I won't stand for this crap."

At first, neither one of us says a word.

"*He* did," Bobby says. "He said he hates the Yankees."

"He hates the Yankees? That's what this is about? And let me guess... He hates the Yankees because he *loves* the Red Sox and you *hate* the Red Sox," Mick says.

"That about covers it," Bobby admits.

"Jimmy? Is that what happened?"

"It happened so fast that I guess that's the story," I respond.

"Okay. So shake this off and forget about it. Yankees. Red Sox. Mets. Phillies. We're not on those teams, right? We're part of The Expos organization, understand? And you two are on the same *team*. You know what a team is? You've played on teams before, right?"

We both nod in agreement, but stay silent.

"Good. We have that straight," Mick says. "Grow up! You're old enough to wear a cup, act like it! Get dressed, and get out on that field. You'll find out what the line-up is in a couple of minutes. Maybe you'll even be in it."

I look at Mangino. He's still looking at the floor. I pick up my stuff and put on my shirt. Expos farm team shirt. Bailey, number 11 on the back.

I walk out onto the field, Mangino walking behind me.

"Welcome, pilgrim," says Skip. "So nice of you to join us."

He calls everyone over to a big huddle to announce the line-up for today's scrimmage.

"Okay, listen up," he says. "We got 34 players on this roster and nine positions to fill, so some of you are going to be my companions in the dug-out for the game, some will be in the bullpen. Don't be insulted if you're not playing. It's a long season.

"So here we go.

"Russ, you're the starting catcher. On first, Logan, second, McKenna, third, Tidwell, short, Golden. Left, I want Jefferson, center, Jakubowski, and Arroyo in right. Starting pitcher is Prescott. I want the rest of the pitchers in the bullpen, and the other two catchers out there, too.

"Everyone got it? I don't want to hear any grumbling. That's it for today. We'll talk about things later. Or you can come to me privately."

I'm kind of glad I'm not starting. I think I could be a reliever, but I'm not sure I could start.

I overhear some of the other guys talking about Bud. "He thinks he's hot stuff," one says. "Let's see what happens today, when he has to face real batters."

For God's sake, the guy just came back from his grandmother's funeral. Give him a break. He's the best we've got.

I keep walking.

The other two catchers are lumbering out to the bullpen, laden with their gear. The leg protectors make them walk bow-legged. They have their ball-caps on backwards, with the bill facing down their necks.

Johnny Forsythe from Birmingham, Alabama, and Stevie Long from Utica, New York, couldn't be more different. Johnny is what my dad might call "classic catcher"—short, stocky, broad shoulders, showing broken teeth when he smiles. Stevie, on the other hand, is tall and lean, and my dad might ask how he could stand to squat behind the plate for more than a couple of innings. But he seems calm and flexible, just as a tall man should be, to be a successful catcher.

"Hey, Jimmy!" Johnny calls out. "You wanna toss a few when we get to the 'pen?"

"Sure," I reply. "I'm getting a little antsy, anyway."

He gives me a missing-teeth grin. The catcher's mask doesn't always protect a guy from taking a ball or even a bat in the teeth. That's why catchers have to be tough as nails, my dad always said. "And it doesn't hurt to be a little dense, if you're looking at a 90-mile-an-hour fast ball, trying to catch it, and get out of the way at the same time," he'd say.

The other guys are just milling around.

I play with my cap. It's made of a heavier wool than any other cap I've worn, and it's itchy in the back. Maybe that's why some of the guys wear their hair a little long. Mine is cut really short, because I sweat so much when I pitch.

The bullpen is dry and dusty. The little "mound" is just a slightly raised pile of dirt with a ten-inch-long pitching rubber worked deeply into it. The rubber is 60.5 feet from home plate, just like the real distance from the pitcher's mound to the plate.

Johnny settles himself in his crouch, sets a target for me with his over-sized catcher's mitt, and says, "Let 'er rip!"

Warm up, Dad says, warm up. Don't do anything that would hurt your arm or your rotator cuff. That's a hard one to heal, that rotator cuff. I've seen guys...

I say, "No, I'm going to throw a few easy ones to warm up. Okay?"

"Othay," it sounds like he says, his mask muffling his Southern accent.

After a few of these, Johnny stands up, flips the mask back, and says, "You okay now to throw some heat?"

"Yeah," I reply. "I'm ready."

I look over my left shoulder to see if I can see a phantom runner at first base. This is my routine; I know no one's there, but it's just what I do. Since no one's there, I steady my back foot—my right foot—on the rubber. I bring my left foot up to my chest to get velocity on the pitch, kick it into the air, bring my right arm back just behind my ear, come down on the left foot and let the ball go.

A fast ball.

Johnny catches it and says, "Good velocity, son! Give me a couple more like that!"

So I do. Five heaters in a row. He stands up after each pitch and sends the ball back to me. "I like it," he says.

I look up and Cesar is strolling into the 'pen. He folds his arms across his chest, over his big belly. The Buddha of baseball.

"Gimme some breaking stuff," Johnny says, as he gets back down into his crouch.

I can see the plate clearly from where I stand. I'm not all that tall—6'2"—but I have a good view from the mound. I do the routine thing again, of looking at a non-existent runner at first base, then I go into my wind-up, my leg kick, bring my arm back with two fingers over the two seams on the ball, almost as if I were going to throw a two-seam fastball. But when I let it go, I cock my wrist to the left to get the breaking action on the curve. If I don't do that correctly, it won't drop or break, especially into a left-handed batter.

The first one I throw breaks properly, but it most likely would have hit a right-handed batter, or at least brushed him back from the plate. It might have fooled a left-hander into taking a wild swing. A good pitch.

The second one does not break at all, and any good hitter sends that one over the fence. I catch a look at Cesar, and he's shaking his head, saying something like, "Umm, umm, umm, no, no, no, *hijo.*"

I'm trying too hard.

I'm overthinking, in Bud's words.

I close my eyes. *Think of Fenway Park. Think Bill Monbouquette. Think Dave Morehead. Think Dick Radatz. Okay. Let's go.*

I open my eyes and look ahead. I see Johnny squatting, giving me a target with his dusty, oversized glove. *I can do this.* I catch a glimpse of Cesar. *Why does he intimidate me?*

I put the ball in my glove, but I'm still holding it in my right hand, rolling it around inside the pocket, caressing the round sphere, to show the white leather and red stitching how much I love it, how much it should depend on me to become something, as I depend on it to make me something. We have a symbiotic relationship, like a periwinkle on a piece of driftwood on the sand at Wessagusset Beach.

I feel the leather and the tiny pieces of dirt that have built up within the stitches. *Okay. I've got this.*

Johnny is pounding his glove. "C'mon, Jimmy, right here, Jimmy!"

I lean back on the rubber with my right foot, bring my left leg back, bend my left knee, take my right hand out of the glove, drop my gloved hand by my side, kick the left leg up, bring the right arm back, land on the left leg, and release the ball. This time, it breaks exactly the way I want it to—away from the phantom right-hander who's not at the plate, but who would be during a game.

Yessssss!!!!

Johnny stands up and leans his mask up a little so that I can see his mouth. "That's the way I like it!" he says. "If anyone can hit that..."

Cesar saunters over to my would-be mound. "Bravo, Bos-tone. If *chew* can keep that up without hurting *chore* arm, *chew* will be good. It's my *yob* to make sure *chew* find out how not to hurt *chorself.*"

Whew. Big hurdle. I can feel sweat dripping down my face, but it's not really even hot. Tense-sweat. *That's what Dad calls this—tense sweat.*

"I'm all ears, Cesar," I say. I try not to grin too big. Johnny is holding onto the ball and nodding, giving me some sort of approval for the way I was throwing. He seems like he's got his head on straight.

I go to sit on the bullpen bench and let out a big sigh. Richie Newman, another righthander, was already sitting there. He's from California, so we are kind of diametrically opposed, coast-wise. I make a judgment: He's probably one of those laid-back surfer dudes who doesn't feel anxiety.

"It's kind of funny that he calls you 'Bos-tone,' isn't it?" Richie asks. "What's he gonna call me? Beach Boy?" We both laugh. Then he hits my glove with his. Bi-coastal meeting of the minds.

"Your first time away from home?" he asks.

"Yeah. I mean, I've traveled to play ball, but my dad was always with me."

"Yeah, it's not the same," he comments, "even if you're living with a family. You living with a family here?"

"Yeah, the Andersons. They're pretty typical, but I gotta say, the dad is kinda like Archie Bunker."

"Archie Bunker? Must be a laugh and a half!"

"Well, sort of," I say. "You never have to wonder what he's thinking, that's for sure."

Cesar calls us out from under the safety of the bullpen overhang.

"*Mis hijos!*" he says. "We're about to get ready for this game. *Chew* gonna be ready to play when we get to Geneva? We gonna beat them, *entiende*? Understand? We gotta get a good start. The southern boy is going to start today, but *chew* guys probably gonna pitch today, too. Ready? Ready? Ready?"

ALL of us will pitch today? How ridiculous is THAT? Bud will start, pitch to what, six batters, and then each of us pitches to what, two or three batters? Doesn't make sense to me.

"*Chew* will see what Skip, he likes," Cesar says. "This is just a scrimmage, but it's an important game. Pay attention! Very serious today!"

He turns around and walks to the end of the bullpen, clipboard in his hand. He works a phantom beard, mumbling to himself in inaudible Spanish, with a few names punctuating his words. "Wilson? Bailey? Malone? Mangino? Lincoln?"

Is this the order in which he plans to put each of us into this game? He has seen us all throw. What will influence his decisions? Does he make the decision, or will Skip? Right-hander? Left-hander? Sinker-baller? Fast-baller?

This isn't easy for any of us on the field.

CHAPTER 16

Geneva

The bus pulls into Geneva, sputtering diesel fumes and letting off steam from the brakes. Our close to three dozen healthy young men get off the bus, checking out the field and parking lot. Some yawn and stretch, to work out the kinks from the 170-mile trip on winding back roads.

Geneva seems a bit of a backwater town, like Jamestown. The most exciting place is the big race track at Watkins Glen, and that's a seasonal thing.

A guy from the home team with a clipboard calls us together, barks out a few orders, then points us to the visitors' locker room. We grab our duffel bags and head over. No one wants to be feeling road-weary when they're on the ball field, so we keep stretching along the way.

One of the Geneva guys takes off his hat to scratch his head as he sizes up our team. He's dark and tanned, not very tall, and he glances over his shoulder at me, squinting his eyes, focusing on me.

Gotta be Valderrama. Cesar said to look at him you'd think he was nothing, average-looking guy, but he can hit the ball way over the fences.

Cesar told us Fidel Castro was a stellar baseball player in his time, before the Cuban Revolution, and that Castro was livid when Valderrama defected. *Guess he had big plans for that boy. Guess the Senators do, too.*

Members of the Geneva team make their way into the ballpark, some walking as if on a mission, others as if they weren't worried about whether they played that day or not.

I am, in the words of my mother, a basket case. You're going to hell in a handbasket, The Filly would say. Yup. That's how I feel. How can they be so calm?

I head in that direction, and Johnny comes up behind me, knocking me lightly on the rear end with the back of his glove.

"Hey! What're you doing, sizing up the opposition?" he asks.

Reality check.

"Uh, oh, don't do it," Johnny advises. "You'll get yourself so worked up that your curve ball won't break!"

"Yeah, yeah, I know, I know. I was just thinking that this is the first game I will ever be in that my dad won't be in the stands."

"It's a whole new world for all of us," he says, in his Alabama drawl. "It ain't bad enough that we're in this backwater town, is it? We cain't look up in the stands and see the people we've always known, huh?"

He puts his arm around me as we walk into the park's visiting team entrance.

As Skip calls us together in the locker room, he barks, "Listen up. Y'all know the starting lineup. I'm not going over that again. All remaining pitchers out in the bullpen with two catchers—Johnny and Stevie—be out there to warm them up if I need them.

"Cesar will be out there, too. Now, you might have to warm up and you might not get in the game. Don't read anything into that. I'm not here to be your psychiatrist—or your mommy. Got it?"

Heads nod.

"Good. Now, this is a team, right? You do what I say, not what you feel like doing. You've all played this game since before you were born..."

Chuckles and some groans from the team and the coaches.

"Yeah, yeah, you have. You wouldn't be here if you hadn't. That's how you get noticed. Baseball's in your DNA.

"Doesn't mean I don't think you're gonna make mistakes. Doesn't mean I think you're ready to step onto the major league express tomorrow. No way. No how. What it means is that I expect you to listen to the coaching staff and me. And you should be expecting a lot of yourselves as well. Got it?"

Heads nod again, this time more together.

"Any questions?"

Silence.

"Okay. Let's get out there."

Bud comes up from behind me and pats my butt. "It's real now, kiddo," he says. "Let's go get 'em."

"I've got butterflies just to know my dad won't be there, and I'll..."

"Oh, cut the crap! Do you think your dad would want you to act this way? Straighten up, walk how he taught you. Did he have HIS dad at every game HE pitched? Do this BECAUSE he's not here, FOR him," Bud said.

"Got it," I reply. *Shoulders straight. Take control. Walk with confidence. You got this. That's what Dad would say. And do.*

Bud puts his arm around me, his left hand loosely covered by his well-worn glove, hanging halfway down my shoulder. "You're okay, Bos-tone, you're okay," he says, smiling at me. "Besides," he adds, "your dad might not be here, but my grandma is. I *feel* her."

Me too, now that he mentions it.

CHAPTER 17

Batter Up!

B ud's on the mound, warming up with Russ. The infielders are simulating ground balls and pop-ups to each other—Al Logan at first to Nick Golden at shortstop, Joey Tidwell at third to Donnie McKenna at second.

The outfielders are throwing long line drives to one another—Donnie Jefferson in left, Tim Jakubowski in center, and Dave Arroyo in right.

They look like a real team, not just guys with matching uniforms who showed up and chose sides for a pick-up game.

The umpires show up. One behind the plate, one at first base, one at third. All look very young, but I bet they think that about us as well.

Skip meets the Geneva manager behind home plate to exchange line-ups with the home plate umpire.

Pitchers not in the game, of which I am one, are already in the bullpen, along with two catchers and Cesar, hanging over the bullpen fence, waiting to start.

Over the crackling PA system, I hear tapping on a microphone followed by loud, grating feedback. "Ladies and gentlemen, welcome to Geneva, New York, home of the Geneva Senators. Today's non-league game features our hometown team taking on the Jamestown Falcons.

"Now, please stand for our National Anthem."

An outdated recording of a John Phillip Sousa-type version of "The Star Spangled Banner" is played through the loudspeaker.

"...and the land of the freeeeee....and the home....of the...brave!"

Maybe 400 people are at the ballpark, in addition to the two teams. It's not exactly empty, but it's certainly not full. This game isn't on the regular schedule, so it may well have been a surprise to many of the team's faithful to even have a game today.

When it's our turn to pitch in the bottom of the first, leading off for Geneva is Luis Munoz, and if he gets on base, he's been known to steal a base or two. Bud is ready for him. He sets and pitches. Russ calls for a fastball.

"STRIKE ONE!" calls the umpire—no swing from Munoz.

Next pitch. Bud and Russ decide on a curve ball. "BALL!" says the ump.

Bud leans over and looks for a sign from Russ. He stands up straight and sends a fastball in, high and tight. Munoz catches a piece of it, pops the ball up in the infield, right at Randy at second, who makes the catch.

One down.

Up next is Randy Wilson. Lefty. Spray hitter. Can hit to all fields. Good, level swing. Bud looks him over. Russ is tilting his head back and forth. Only he and Bud know what that means. Bud sets and pitches. Curve ball. Doesn't break exactly the way Bud expects, but Wilson swings, anyway.

"STRIKE ONE!"

Russ sends the ball back to Bud. He gets back into his crouch and sends a signal to Bud against his left leg. Bud gets it. Fastball. Down and in. Bud throws the agreed-upon pitch. Wilson swings, sending the ball fowl.

"STRIKE TWO!"

Bud and Russ figure they should put the ball exactly where that last one was. Bud sends the ball to the plate. Wilson fouls it off. Count remains at 0–2.

Wilson starts to kick the dirt in the batter's box. He stomps both feet with his cleats, stirring up dirt and white line paint. He's ready again.

Bud sends a curve ball that breaks away from Wilson, but he makes contact, and it dribbles on the ground, much like a bunt, down the third base line. Joey Tidwell shows amazing speed and runs in to get the ball. Tidwell's fast—and he gets the ball and throws Wilson out by half a step at first base.

And now Bud must face Yulias Valderrama, The Cuban who is taking the United States baseball world by storm. Everyone mentions the word "phenom" in connection with him.

Bud circles the mound, kicks some of the dirt. His toes make the reddish-looking soil fly up to his knees. He puts his hands on his hips and gets on top of the mound, then sets his right foot on the rubber, bending at the waist so that he can look at Russ, who's gone into his crouch, for a sign.

Russ taps the left top side of his mask, then gives Bud two fingers to the right side of his right leg. *Fastball.*

Valderrama does not swing at the first pitch. Good rule of thumb.

"STRIKE ONE!" yells the umpire.

Valderrama thought it was low. It wasn't. It was right down the pike, straight down the middle in the strike zone. Valderrama probably could have hit it into downtown Geneva if he had taken a swing.

The Cuban digs his heels in, mutters, *"Ay, dios mio,"* shakes his head, gets focused in the batter's box. He stares at Bud with an intensity Bud's never seen in a batter before. His brown eyes say, "Okay, come and get me, but I have all the weapons. All of them. You will not win."

Russ puts two fingers in the air in the form of a "V" to indicate that there are two outs as he settles behind the plate. The Cuban is incensed at this. *What does he mean? Que es eso? No me diga!*

Russ goes back into his crouch, gives another sign to Bud, and the umpire is ready. The Cuban digs in again, almost drawing his strategy with his cleats into the dirt. He looks up again at Bud with the same intensity as before.

Bud thinks, "Does he practice that look in the mirror every day?" Then he chuckles to himself.

The Cuban gets more and more angry when Bud lets out that little snicker. *Es el tiempo para un jonrón.*

Russ calls for another fastball. Bud sends it to the same place as the first one.

The Cuban is ready. He takes a textbook swing, following through from low to high, giving the ball a rocket-like ride over the fence.

Bud is impressed.

As The Cuban jogs around the bases, he looks over at Bud, who is actually admiring his hit, and gives him the bullfighter stare again. As he hops onto home plate, scoring the first run of the game, he turns and looks at Bud again.

Bud shakes his head, laughs at himself for throwing that pitch, vows never to throw another one like that to Valderrama, and looks over at the visitors' dugout. He catches The Cuban's eye and gives him a fleeting "thumbs-up" sign.

The Cuban is not accustomed to receiving an opposing player's accolades. He jumps out of the dugout, yelling at Bud, but Bud has no idea what he means, because it's all in Spanish. The umpire tells him to get back in the dugout.

One of the other players on his team tells The Cuban in Spanish that it's okay, that the guy was only trying to compliment his hit, but The Cuban doesn't seem to believe that an opposing pitcher does such a thing. His teammate tells him in Spanish that sometimes this happens in the United States. The Cuban's not buying it.

The next Geneva batter strikes out.

After one full inning, it's Geneva 1, Jamestown nothing.

Those of us in the bullpen have no idea what happened, except for the fact that one of the Geneva batters hit a home run off Bud. Cesar tells us to relax, it's only one an inning, but I keep thinking it rattled Bud.

Four innings go by, and Bud's still on the mound. Our batters have answered with four runs, so now, after four complete, it's Jamestown 4, Geneva 1.

Cesar says, "*Chew*! Bos-tone! Start warming up! And *chew*! New-man! *Chew* too!"

Johnny gets up to work with me, and Stevie Long puts on his gear so that he can warm up Richie Newman.

There are two pitching rubbers in the bullpen, but the mounds are just little piles of dirt.

"Nice and easy," Cesar says. "Don't throw hard yet. *Chew* need to relax and find a rhythm. *Ches*. Nice and easy."

Richie and Stevie talk for a few minutes while Stevie adjusts the straps on his chest protector. I hear them laugh a little.

"Hey, Bos-tone!" Cesar yells at me. "*Chew* worry too much. Relax, relax, relax. Johnny-boy, make him relax. *Chew* good at that." Then he walks up and down, from Johnny to me, from me to Johnny, to look at my mechanics. "*Chew* lookin' pretty good today, Bos-tone. Relax, relax, relax."

In the top of the fifth, despite a lead-off walk, the score remains the same.

A mild roar goes out from the small crowd. In the bottom of the fifth, with one out and runners at first and third, one of the Geneva players hit into an inning-ending double play, shortstop to second to first base. Classic. Nice work, guys.

Bud has now pitched five innings, and the only real mistake he made was the fastball to The Cuban.

"New-man! Oh, New-man!" Cesar calls out, almost singing Richie's name. "You're going in! Get *chore* stuff!"

Richie looks at me as he's opening the latch on the bullpen fence. "One coast, represents!" he says. "The other coast goes next!" Then he smiles at me and gives me a military-like salute off the top of his cap.

Off he goes, hopping and skipping to the mound on the field, to try to hold onto Bud's lead.

In the bottom of the sixth, Richie gives up two singles but strikes out two, and gets the final out on a fly ball to center. Still Jamestown 4, Geneva 1.

Our guys pick up one more run in the top of the sixth, when Geneva brings in a reliever who doesn't seem to have much control. He walks two, one steals a base, then we get a sacrifice to bring in the run, and he strikes out two, to end the inning. Hot and cold pitcher, my dad would say.

Richie stays in for the bottom of the seventh. On his fifth pitch, the Geneva batter sends a bullet of a line drive that hits him in the leg, and he goes down. The batter gets a single, but Richie can't get up. Russ rushes to the mound, joined by Skip, Mick, Finn, Joey and Frankie. Cesar sees what happened and yells, "*Valgame, Dios!*" and runs out to the mound.

We hang over the edge of the bullpen fence, silent. It could be any of us on that mound.

Richie still doesn't move.

An ambulance screams into the park, three guys pushing a stretcher onto the field. They carefully move Richie onto it and wheel him out to the ambulance and place him in the back.

He's off to the hospital.

Cesar trudges back to the bullpen, out of breath. "Those *médicos*, they did not want him to move," he says. "Don't know if his leg is broken. Very sore," he adds.

Chew! Bos-tone! Get out there!"

Yes, I am warmed up. Yes, I knew I would be pitching today. But after *that?*

I feel my shoulders rise and fall with the breath entering my diaphragm. I adjust my hat and start making my way to the mound, as ready as I'll ever be. Gotta do this for Richie. The other coast.

Russ walks out to the mound. "He'll be okay," he reassures me. "I told him not to get up, to wait until he got checked out.

"So listen...Here are the signs...same ones you used in the bullpen. Got it?"

"Yep."

I look up in the stands, as I always do. Of course, my dad isn't there. I see an old guy about six rows behind our dugout, with a scorecard in his hand. I focus on him. He's my dad today.

I shake out my shoulders and put the ball in my glove. I work it around a little before I throw a few pitches to Russ. *Nice and easy. Nice and easy. Don't want to give anything away. Runner on first. No outs. Listen to Russ. Watch what he calls for. Pay attention. Focus.*

"Batter up!" the umpire yells.

It's Luis Munoz, and I have to remind myself that he's fast. Right-handed, but can get out of the box pretty quickly if he gets on base. Then it's Randy Wilson, and I watched him during batting practice. Then I'll have to face The Cuban.

Over thinking again. I look over at the dugout, where Bud leans on the railing. He mouths, "You got it!"

Russ calls for a fastball. I lean down, coddle the ball, rock back on the pitching rubber, pull my left foot up in a perpendicular motion, bring my right arm back, and fire.

Munoz hits a ground ball to second base. Donnie scoops it up, throws to Joey who steps on second, but Munoz is too fast. Fielder's choice. One out, runner on first.

Wilson steps up to the left side of the plate. He's grinning from ear to ear, because he couldn't hit Bud, but now wants to destroy me. Munoz is fast and could probably score on a single. If Wilson can hit a double, he gets into scoring position, then it's The Cuban's turn to hit a slammer off me.

Russ calls for a curve ball to start. I shake him off. He jumps out of his crouch and comes to the mound. "What the hell?" he says. "You're supposed to do what I say! I'm the captain of this ship! I say throw a curve, you throw a curve!"

"I've only thrown one pitch in a game here. I'm not sure it will break yet. Let me throw a fastball here and then a curve."

He shakes his head. "No. I say curve, you throw a curve. That's it. Capeesh?"

"Okay, I follow."

He trots back behind the plate and crouches, patting his huge catcher's glove a few times and setting up the target.

I throw what is supposed to be a curve. It doesn't break and it's in the dirt. Russ is able to trap it.

"BALL ONE!"

Wilson looks at me with that grin again.

Russ says fastball this time.

I give it all I've got. I throw a heater, and it almost knocks Russ over. Wilson swings and misses.

"STRIKE ONE!"

The grin is now gone from Wilson's face. But now he knows I can do that. He's reading me. He's looking me up and down.

Russ calls for a curve again. I inhale deeply and sigh, feeling my shoulders rise and fall as I throw the pitch. It's low and breaks to the outside of the plate. Wilson reaches out and punches it into short right field. Donnie starts waving his arms and yelling, "I got it! I got it!"

Wilson pops out. Munoz stays on first. Two outs.

Now it's The Cuban.

He stands in, burrowing his feet in the batter's box. His intense stare goes right through me, as if he'll get the scarlet cape out of my hands without any problem, and gore me before I can use the *estoca*, because he thinks I don't know what I'm doing.

He swings the bat a few times in my direction.

Russ calls for a curve. *Start this guy off with a curve? Why? But he's the boss, the captain of this ship.*

So I throw a curve, and it breaks exactly the way I want it to, but this guy sends it foul, high into the seats. He's transmitting a direct message to me: Don't mess with me, boy-o. I can hit anything you can send.

"STRIKE ONE!"

Russ says fastball this time. He gives me a hint: high and tight. Okay. High and tight it is.

I let go of a fastball, high and tight, and it brushes The Cuban back from the plate. Now he thinks I'm throwing at him. Now he's really going for the fences.

"BALL ONE!"

Russ says fastball again. I throw it, and I watch the ball sail over my head into the stratosphere, to the moon, to Saturn, to Pluto. It's gone—a two-run homer for The Cuban.

Out of the corner of my eye, I see Skip making his way to the mound. Russ joins him. "Do you think you can get this last guy out?" Skip asks. "I mean, we're still up by two."

"He's throwing pretty good, Skip," says Russ, talking about me as if I'm not there. "Let's go one more batter."

"Okay, one more. Let's see what happens." He pats me on the butt and heads back to the dugout. Bud looks over at me from the railing and mouths the words, "Hang in, hang in."

I face Luke Benson, from Armpit, Texas, where all they do is hit balls and chase cows. Every ball he hit during batting practice left the stadium.

He strolls to the batter's box.

"C'mon," he says to me, with his Texas drawl, "throw me one of those. I like *those*!"

Russ is not happy. He calls for a curve. I lean back and play with the ball in my glove for a few seconds, trying to convince it to do what I want.

I send the curve ball to the plate. It's low, but it breaks, and Benson swings.

"STRIKE ONE!"

Benson looks directly at me. "So you makin' me look like a fool, huh, boy?"

Russ tells him to shut up.

"Zip it, crouch boy!" he says to Russ.

The umpire warns if they keep it up, they'll both be thrown out of the game.

Russ wants another curve ball. I guess that will throw him off. So I send another curve to the plate.

Benson swings again, irate. He takes a couple of steps toward me, as the umpire yells "STRIKE TWO!" He shakes his head and digs his cleats into the dirt.

Russ calls for a fastball, but this time he signals that he wants it to be right at the letters. I'm not sure I can be that precise, but I do my best.

I look up at the guy in the stands who's my dad for the day. He gives me a nod and I nod back.

Fastball. At the letters. Benson swings and fouls it off. Still 0–2.

Russ says fastball again, so I throw another one, and I make it the fastest heater I can.

"STRIKE THREE!"

Benson caught looking. He slams down his bat and starts screaming at the umpire. "You call that a strike? What the hell?" And he starts kicking dirt at the ump. *I've heard most of those words before, from pissed-off Boston drivers.*

"You're OUTTA HERE!" says the umpire.

Benson kicks dirt all the way back to the home dugout.

End of seven. Jamestown 5, Geneva 3.

Cesar decides to send in John Jordan from Tennessee to close the last inning. After a rocky start, giving up a lead-off double and a walk, he gets a double play and a pop-up to end the game.

Jamestown 5, Geneva 3.

We wait for news of Richie from the hospital. We all know that the Geneva batter didn't hit the line drive at Richie on purpose.

The season already feels long.

CHAPTER 18

Conversation with Dad

When I get back to the Anderson house that night, I ask Mrs. Anderson if I can use the phone to call home. "I can make it a collect call," I say.

"Jimmy, honey, you don't have to do that. Just call them," she says.

I make my way over to the little L-shaped mahogany phone table. The phone sits on the top shelf, and the phone books sit neatly underneath on the table part.

The phone has a rotary dial, and a short cord. The Andersons have not gone with touch tone yet, but then, neither have the Baileys back in Weymouth.

I dial our home number. My mother answers.

"Jimmy? Is that you? Are you all right? You don't call us much! Why don't you call more?"

"Well, Ma, we're kinda busy, and we travel a lot, and I have to get a lot of sleep."

"I can't tell you how much I hate baseball!" she says. "This is *exactly* why I didn't want your father to play professionally! And I'm not sure that I want you playing ball for a living, either!"

"Ma, I..."

"Oh, I'm sure you want to talk to your father!" she says. "James! Your son is on the phone, and he wants to speak to *you* instead of *me*..."

I can hear the television blaring in the background. I wonder what he's watching, and I wonder if he and Mr. Archie Bunker Anderson would get along, even for a little while.

"Jimmy? Is that you?" Dad asks, when he picks up the receiver. "How's it going?"

75

"I'm doing fine, I think," I say. "Just wanted to let you know that I pitched today."

"Okay…How'd it go?"

"Well, I wasn't the starter, I was relief for a guy who took a line drive in the leg. We don't know yet if his leg is broken. It was pretty bad. He went down and couldn't get up."

"Saw that many times myself," Dad says. "How did it go for you?"

"Well, it was stressful, to say the least, but I've got a good catcher, so he got me through it. It was tough going in when they were taking Richie out in an ambulance, though. For the first few pitches, all I could think about was what happened and how he was lying on the ground for so long and couldn't move."

"How many times do I have to tell you that you need to focus on yourself when you're on the mound?" Dad asks. "It's not about what's happening around you or who's watching you. It's about you and your catcher. How many times have I told you that?"

"I know, I know, but it was hard to do here. If you'd been in the stands…"

"The stands might as well have been empty!" Dad says. "I'm in a ship-yard, for God's sake, so you can be there! Don't forget it!"

"I won't, Dad. I think about that all the time."

"Good. That's the way it should be. That's what dads are for. What else is up?"

"Everyone here is really good. Stars in their hometowns, too," I point out.

"They'd never be drafted if they wasn't," Dad says. "So you're past opening day now. It's uphill from here. And your coaches? Do you get along with them?"

"Yeah. Except today was just a scrimmage. You know the pitching coach, Cesar Dominguez? He calls me 'Bos-tone.'"

Dad laughs.

"He always had a great sense of humor. He was in the minors with me."

"You knew him in the minors?"

"Yup. He was a terrific pitcher in his day, but back then he couldn't speak a lick of English. He liked to swear at the umpires in Spanish."

We both laugh. I try to picture Cesar without his Santa Claus belly, with a lean, athletic body, mumbling Spanish swear words under his breath at bad calls.

"Must have been a sight, Dad, must have been a sight," I say.

"Yes, it was, Jimmy."

I sigh. I know he wishes he was me. Instead, he's listening to me, about 600 miles away from home, tell him that I was rattled—rather than ready—ready to take on the world by facing any batter who stepped into that box. Like he was.

I am not that pitcher. I strive to be that man, but I am nowhere near there.

CHAPTER 19

The Real Opening Day

The next day, the locker room is buzzing, guys chuckling about yesterday's win.

"Yeah, it was just a scrimmage."

"A win's a win, man."

But what if we lose Richie? He's a solid pitcher, set-up guy.

I'm pacing. Bud puts his arm on my shoulder.

"Hey, kiddo, what's up?"

I shrug, as I put one foot on a bench to pull up my sock.

"I'm so worried about Richie. Not good, not good."

"It didn't look good, especially from where I sat," says Bud.

He takes his hand away from where it was draped over my arm. For the first time, he looks square-jawed to me, almost stern.

He stares down the line at the guys who were fooling around.

He has enough on his plate. He just lost his beloved grandmother. And I want to give him my troubles? Am I THAT selfish? Maybe I am.

Skip and Mick enter the locker room. We go into run silent, run deep mode.

"Listen up!" Skip barks. "Update on Richie. He stayed in the hospital overnight."

"He'll be out sometime today. Nothing broken. He's got a technicolor bruise on his leg from the top of his thigh to the tip of his toes—and a big ole dent in his leg bone where the ball hit. He'll be out for a while, but he'll be working with the trainer."

Cesar strolls in. "*Chew* know, *hijos*, that the surfer dude will steel sit in the bullpen with *chew* all. *Chew* don't have to worry. He be okay."

Richie is going to be okay. But I can't imagine what kind of pain he's in. Wait—did Cesar just call him 'the surfer dude?' He owes me five bucks!

I chuckle a little to myself. *Wait 'til I tell Richie.*

We move on to opening day, and we're playing the Williamsport Red Sox, from Williamsport, Pennsylvania. If I'd signed with the Red Sox, that's the team I'd be playing on.

Skip addresses us, "Based on what Cesar and I have seen during practice and the scrimmage, we've decided on our starting pitching rotation. Y'all probably knew Prescott would be our starter on opening day."

Bud's blushing a little, but Skip is right. We all knew it. Bud was lights out in that scrimmage against Geneva, and no one—with the only possibility of Jerry Malone from Mississippi, who was also vying for the job—thought otherwise.

"As for our number two, three and four in the rotation, Cesar and I agree that it will be Malone, Gibson and McManus. In that order. If that doesn't work, we have other ideas, but that's it. Everyone else is in the bullpen.

"Starting lineup today will be pretty much the way we've been practicing. Hitting lead-off is Tidwell, batting second is Arroyo, then McKenna, batting clean-up is Logan, then Milkewicz, then Jefferson, Golden, then Brindisi, then finally Prescott. Got it?"

Yup. We got it, Skip. We're ready. As ready as we're gonna be.

"The rest of you pitchers and the other two catchers—head to the 'pen as soon as the anthem is over. No complaints. I wanna win a ballgame today. Got it?"

Everyone has his own glove, with different stages of wear and tear. Some need new lacing; some are the color of dirt-covered mahogany, while others are more caramel-colored, with streaks of red-clay dirt worked into the pocket.

Mine is a cafe-au-lait brown, heavy on the au-lait. I still see where my father used a nail and etched "Jimmy B, Jr." just below the glove's heel. I've restitched the thumb webbing more than once.

"Ladies and gentlemen. Welcome to opening day here, as your Jamestown Falcons take on the Williamsport Red Sox, in what will be an exciting contest in the New York-Penn League. Please stand for the singing of the National Anthem."

Today, we have a "live" person singing The Star-Spangled Banner. A woman older than my mother steps onto the field with a crackly microphone. She looks like she should be home baking us cookies instead of singing the Anthem, but she sounds pretty good.

"...and the land of the freeeeeeee....And...the...home...of...the... brave!"

The small crowd claps and cheers as she waves and walks off the field, past our dugout and up the stairs to a seat that has been reserved for her. As she passes, I'm still thinking about homemade cookies.

The public address announcer gives the starting lineups for both teams, and we pitchers are slowly making our way to the bullpen, along with catchers Johnny and Stevie. Richie is with us, still hobbling a little. The trainer thinks he'll be ready to throw off the low mound in a couple of weeks.

Bud throws his warm-up pitches to Russ. He doesn't know it, but his mom and dad are in the stands. They have traveled from Georgia to watch him pitch in his first official game. His mom told Cesar and Skip, but she asked them not to spill the beans, or so Cesar told us as we headed for the bullpen.

Are my dad and The Filly here? What about Donna and Debbie? I don't even know if I'll get into this game. It's obvious they don't think I'm good enough to be a starter. What will my dad think?

"Batter UP!" the umpire commands, and the first batter for the Red Sox is a left-hander who enters the box with a lot of confidence—and a big bat.

Bud sizes him up and looks for a sign from Russ. *Fastball.*

Bud leans back and goes into his motion, firing a fastball right down the pike and into Russ's glove.

"STRIKE ONE!"

The batter doesn't swing. It looks as if he didn't even see the ball until it had been in Russ's glove for a good two or three seconds.

Russ calls for another fastball. Bud rocks back on the pitching rubber and delivers another blazing pitch.

The batter swings later and fouls it off.

"STRIKE TWO!"

The batter seems to be off balance at this point. The count is 0–2, and he seems almost dizzy at the hands of Bud's fastball. But now he's expecting another one.

Russ calls for a curve, just to shake things up.

Bud holds the ball in his glove, twirling it around between the leather and his fingers, caressing and communicating with it so that it will do what he commands it to. He looks down at the ball and telepathically orders it to break sharply so that this batter won't be able to hit it.

Bud goes into his motion, and the ball breaks precisely the way he wants it to, so the batter hits it weakly on the ground to first base, and Logan handles it on his own.

Out number one.

The next batter strikes out, and the third one pops out to Joey at third.

Three up, three down.

Bud and Russ are great battery-mates for a full five innings, during which he gives up one run and three hits. He walks one batter, but the next guy hits into an inning-ending double play.

As for our hitters, Logan hits a two-run homer, and we score two more runs in the bottom of the fifth. Jamestown 4, Williamsport 0.

Out in the 'pen, the rest of us are getting antsy.

"Man-GEEN-oh!" Cesar yells. "Warm up. NOW!"

Bobby gets up, but neither of the two catchers in the 'pen starts to put on his gear.

"Steee-veee! You warm him up!" Cesar commands.

Stevie gets off the bench and grabs his catching gear. It's obvious he does not want to warm up Mangino. No one wants to work with him. I still don't know why.

"Hurry up!" Mangino says. "Who knows when he'll want me to go in, and I gotta warm up."

"Hold your horses, there, Bobby," Stevie said. "This takes a few minutes. You'll be fine."

Mangino starts pacing. He's more nervous than I am. I can't figure out why. He goes to the short warm-up mound and starts kicking the dirt with the toe of his cleats. He is mouthing something that I can't make it out.

"Okay, *chew yust* slow down and warm up," Cesar says, "No throwing fast, like *chew* do sometimes. Slow. Warm. No fast."

Mangino gets the ball in his hands.

He doesn't take time to get acquainted with the ball, my dad would say. He needs to get to know the ball, as if it were a lovely woman he was taking on a date, my dad would say.

"Man-GEEN-OH!" Cesar says. "This is not a New-*Chork* minute I need *chew* to warm up in! Slow down! Don't want *chew* to hurt *chorself*."

He's throwing pretty well. He has a good fastball and a slowly breaking curve. My dad could help him, but I don't think he wants help. He doesn't want friends. He doesn't want anyone's help. I'm not sure if even he knows what he wants.

Cesar also tells Johnny to warm up Alan Petrie, a righthander from Seattle, Washington, a nice guy. He's a little older than the rest of us—23—because he finished college at Arizona State before exercising his draft option onto this team. He just takes everything in, doesn't say much. He has a great curve ball, but his fastball isn't anywhere nearly as quick and precise as that of some of the younger guys. Alan says he thought he was going be sent to Vietnam, but his draft lottery number turned out to be 326. Mine was 345. Both of us were lucky.

It's the top of the sixth inning and Bud faces one batter, who pops up into the infield. Skip goes out to the mound and takes the ball from Bud. He looks out to the 'pen and signals to Cesar to send in Mangino, who's warmed up and ready to go.

"Man-GEEN-OH! It's *chore* turn!" Cesar says.

Bobby goes over to the bullpen gate and nervously plays with the latch. He can't get it open. Stevie walks over and nonchalantly lifts up the latch with one finger.

Bobby walks out to the mound, where Russ is waiting to hand him the ball.

"Listen up, Mangino, I'm the boss around here," Russ says. "I call for a fastball, you throw a fastball. No taking matters into your own hands. Capeesh?"

"Yup."

"And don't give this ump any lip. He'll throw you out just as soon as look at you," Russ says. "He's a hard ass."

"Yup."

"Just throw what I tell you, and you'll be fine."

"Yup."

Mangino goes to the mound and walks around like a chicken looking for corn feed on the ground. He pounds his feet into the dirt and then finds a spot near the pitching rubber. Russ is standing up, not crouching, just looking at him. He shakes his head a few times, and I'm sure he's rolling his eyes under his mask. The umpire can't see this, but he's also getting impatient.

The Williamsport batter walks into the batter's box and digs in. He's short and stocky, maybe the catcher. I can't tell from the bullpen. We're hanging over the bullpen fence, trying to keep up with Mangino and his pitching. We've only seen him pitch during practices; he didn't throw during the scrimmage, and he's been hot and cold during practice.

Russ has gone into his crouch. Bobby bends at the waist and looks in for a sign. He recognizes the call: *fastball*. He stands up straight and pulls the ball and his glove into his chest. From where I sit, it almost looks as if he's saying a prayer to the gods of baseball. *Please, don't let me screw up. I can't screw this up.*

He stops for a second to straighten out his hat. He takes it off then puts it back on a couple of times, takes a deep breath, and decides it's time to throw the ball. *Fastball.* That's what Russ wants. He brings his left leg up, rocks his right leg back onto the pitching rubber, rears his right arm back with his elbow cocked, and fires, landing on the left leg as he does.

Boom! The ball smacks into Russ's glove with a sound that only a fastball can make. Horsehide hitting glove leather at 95 miles an hour. It's a beautiful thing.

"STRIKE ONE!"

The batter has no idea that the ball even left Bobby's hand. Even Bobby himself has never thrown a ball that fast before. It feels good. But can he do it again?

Bobby takes another mini-tour around the mound, kicking up a little more dirt. He picks up a handful of soil and scatters it back onto the mound, then grinds a little of it into the ball. *Do what I tell you, little ball. Do what I say. Don't take no for an answer.*

He looks in to see what pitch Russ is looking for. *Fastball. Again. Okay. You can do this, little ball. Blind this guy with your speed.*

Pitch number two leaves his hand. It is not anywhere nearly as fast as the first one, he thinks, but the batter fouls it off to the first base side.

"STRIKE TWO!"

Bobby feels sweat dribbling from his hairline, all the way down his right cheek. He uses his right elbow to nudge it away from his mouth.

He leans down at the waist again, with his right hand dangling down by his side and his glove hand behind his back. *Curveball. Break it to the left. Inside.*

Bobby does what Russ calls for, but the ball doesn't break the right way, and it hits the batter on the hands. The batter gets to take first base. He glares at Bobby, as if this was planned. Bobby wants to scream all kinds of expletives his way. *If I wanted to hit you, I would have aimed for your [expletive] head!*

The guys from the Williamsport dugout come up to the top of the steps, as if they're going to come out to the field and pummel Bobby for throwing at their teammate. Their manager, a former player named Roger Donahue, held them back with his hand. "No intent," he assures them. "Stay put."

And they do.

But our guys are just as ready to come out to the field and defend Bobby, even though he doesn't seem to have any friends on this team, and he doesn't seem to care. Just like his counterpart across the diamond, Skip tells everyone to relax.

"Calm down, nothin' to worry about. Got it?"

Those of us in the 'pen are on pins and needles. Did Bobby throw at this guy? Did the guy lean into the pitch so that he'd be hit? Hurts like hell to be hit by a hardball traveling at high speed, but some guys will take one for the team.

No one out, runner on first. The runner keeps rubbing his hand—the one Bobby hit with the pitch—and sneering at Bobby on the mound. Bobby looks over his shoulder at first base. The runner takes a few steps off the bag and starts leaning toward second. He may or may not be looking to steal, but he's trying to throw off Bobby's rhythm. His teammates in the dugout are egging him on.

Bobby touches his chin to his chest and his eyes dart furtively toward first. The next batter enters the box. The batters are a blur to him; all he can differentiate at this point is whether it's a righthander or a lefthander. It's up to Russ to discover any idiosyncrasies in batters.

This batter is a righty. Russ goes into his crouch and signals to Bobby to ignore the runner. But Bobby is obsessed with the guy on first. He throws over to Al, who's holding the runner on, and the runner skiffles back to the bag, smiling at Bobby.

Russ asks for time and goes to the mound. "Bobby," he says, "watch me, not the runner. He's a catcher, for God's sake. He ain't gonna steal a base! He's messin' with you. Let it go. Pitch to the batter. Ignore him. Watch me. Capeesh?"

"Yup. Yup. Yup."

Russ walks back to the plate and pulls his mask down, gets into his crouch, pounds the mitt and gives Bobby a target. The sign? *Curve.*

Bobby takes his time and sends a curve to Russ. Low and outside. But it broke the way it should have.

"BALL ONE!"

The batter pulls the bill of his cap up and down a few times and looks directly at Bobby, trying to get him to look at first base. He's not buying. He's watching Russ, the way he's supposed to. Russ calls for a fastball.

Bobby rears back and sends a blistering bomb to Russ, almost knocking him to the backstop. The batter swings and misses, looking like a helicopter blade as he goes nearly completely around.

"STRIKE ONE!"

Count is one and one. The runner is still flirting with Bobby, playing a cat-and-mouse game at first. Al is holding him on, aiming his big, awkward first baseman's mitt at the mound, in case Bobby decides to throw at the target.

Russ calls for a fastball again. Bobby delivers.

The batter pulls a ground ball to the opposite field, and the runner has to jump to avoid being hit. It goes under Al as he dives to try to trap it, and into right field for a long single for the batter, and the runner—no matter that he's a catcher—makes it all the way to third base.

Runners at the corners, no one out.

Bobby starts hammering the fist of his pitching hand into his glove, muttering to himself. Now what?

He gave up that pitch. The batter pulled it. That's that. Can't cry over spilled milk, his mother would say. His mother might say, "Well, I saw something just like that happen to Whitey Ford, and he just got back on the mound and struck out the side!" *Yeah, Mom, that's my strategy. I'll just go back out there, make believe I'm Whitey Ford and strike out the side! Easy-peasy.*

Russ stands up, flips his mask back, and points to the mound. The umpire yells, "PLAY BALL!"

Okay. Okay. OKAY.

Bobby takes the ball, twirls it around in his glove, then looks at the batter who's now in the box. This guy's also a right-hander, a little taller than the runner on first.

Russ calls for a fastball. Bobby leans back on the rubber and fires. The batter swings at this first pitch and pops it up to the shortstop.

Infield fly rule in play.

One down, runners at the corners.

The next batter is a lefty. He stands in, swinging his bat, low at first, then level a few times. Bobby is looking directly at Russ, not at the batter, who's crowding the plate, almost as if to dare Bobby to throw inside to him and maybe even hit him the way he did the runner who's now on third base.

Russ is rocking back and forth on his heels. He feels the tension too. He can hear the umpire whistling in between pitches. *What the hell is HE so happy about?*

He watches the batter swing, and based on what he sees, he decides: *fastball.*

Bobby does his chicken dance on the mound again, like he's looking for corn in the dirt. He gets the signal from Russ, plays with the ball in his glove, then fires. The ball goes right down the strike zone, and the batter makes contact, hitting a ground ball to second base, but Nick at shortstop bobbles the ball so it's not a double play. The runner from third scores, as the ball turns into an error and an out at first, rather than an inning-ending double play.

Jamestown 4, Williamsport 2. Runner at second base. Two outs.

Bobby glares at Nick. *Why couldn't he make that play? It was a simple ground ball! I should be heading to the dugout and sitting down. Dammit.*

Russ walks out to the mound and puts his arm on Bobby's shoulder.

"Don't touch me!" Bobby yells. "Don't ever touch me!"

"C'mon, man, I'm just trying…"

"Just leave me alone. You're not my shrink. You're not my brother. You're s'pposed to call pitches. That's all."

"Why do you have to be such an asshole?" Russ asks, shaking his head, and walking back toward the plate.

"Just do your job," Bobby says.

Russ turns back as he's walking toward the plate. "Do my job? How about you doing yours?"

The next batter is a righty. He walks around the batter's box the way Bobby scratches at the mound. He points his bat straight at Bobby before he gets into his stance. He stares directly into Bobby's eyes.

Russ wants to call a bad pitch, just to make Bobby look bad. But no. Let's go *fastball.*

He gives Bobby the sign; Bobby nods in agreement, gives a quick glance over to first base and sees the runner is actually on second, behind him. He rocks back and fires a solid fastball, right down the middle, whizzing past the batter.

"STRIKE ONE!"

Russ wonders why he wasn't sent up to Double-A. Probably just because he's a jerk. He settles in. *Fastball*. Again.

Bobby takes a deep breath and fires again. This time, though, the batter makes contact, sending the ball deep into the corner, where it bounces around against the left field wall. The guy from second base scores, and the batter has a double.

Jamestown 4, Williamsport 3. Two down, runner at second.

Bobby bends over, plays with the dirt and throws little handfuls toward Nick at shortstop, but not past the mound itself–just in that direction. Russ knows Bobby doesn't take kindly to words, so, he nods over to Skip, who heads out to Bobby.

"Bobby, what's going on here?" Skip asks. "You're fine, you're fine. You got what it takes to get out of this inning."

"Yup. Yup. Yup."

"Don't give me that shit, Mangino. Is this about pitching or something else?"

"I am pissed off at that last pitch, Skip, that's all. It should have been down and in a little more than it was, and I put it right down the middle, so he jumped on it."

Bobby slams the ball into his glove and walks around for a few seconds as the ump comes out to the mound and tells Skip to break it up.

"Focus, Bobby, focus, and listen to Russ, got it?" Skip says.

"Yup. Yup. Yup," he replies. *I hate Russ, but I will pay attention to what he calls. I wish Stevie were the catcher. He seems to respect me.*

Skip saunters back to the dugout. Al Petrie is warmed up and ready to come in if Bobby screws up.

The next batter is their clean-up guy, a big, right-handed slugger who plays first base. He takes over the whole box, like a race horse engorges the whole stall as he lines up for the Kentucky Derby. A solid single ties the game.

We're hanging over the side of the fence, hoping Bobby can do this. We want Bud to get one in the "w" column.

Russ calls for a curve ball to start things off. Bobby is confused; why not a fastball? He shakes off the sign, but Russ is adamant. Curve ball. *Curve ball, dammit.*

Bobby accepts Russ's order, rears back and fires. The ball breaks, but it's low and outside.

"BALL ONE!"

Slugger-boy looks at Bobby with a wry smile, and then past him to his teammate, who's on second base. He nods his head to his runner, then pulls down the brim of his cap.

Russ calls for a fastball now, which slugger-boy is expecting. Bobby sends a fireball his way, and slugger-boy doesn't even see it until it's landed in Russ's mitt and the umpire calls it.

"STRIKE ONE!"

Russ calls for the curve ball again, and Bobby obliges. The ball breaks from the outside of the plate and into the hitter, brushing him back from the plate, but the umpire calls it–

"STRIKE TWO!"

Slugger-boy looks back at the umpire as if to say that it wasn't a strike, but Russ says nothing. He had moved his mitt slightly to the middle to convince the umpire that Bobby had indeed thrown a strike, even if it might have been marginal. Bobby got the call.

Count is one-two, two outs, runner at second.

Russ calls for a fastball. Bobby's ball jams slugger-boy on the hands, and he pops up the ball to the shortstop, and Nick reels it in.

Inning over. Bobby and Russ walk to the dugout. Normally, Russ would put his arm around his pitcher, but Bobby has commanded him not to touch him. He hopes this is the only inning Bobby pitches in this game.

Petrie comes in for the seventh and eighth innings. Two hits in the seventh, but nothing comes of either of them. Both runners are stranded. Al gets the three batters in order in the eighth, one-two-three.

Our hitters pick up another run in the bottom of the eighth on a double, a ground out, and a sacrifice fly.

Jordan, our closer, takes over in the top of the ninth, and, with runners at first and second and one out, he gets two strike-outs to end the game.

Jamestown, 5, Williamsport, 3. Game over.

It feels like we've won the World Series. Everyone's that happy.

Except Bobby Mangino.

He's off in the corner, sulking.

CHAPTER 20

Post-Game

I clean up my dirty laundry and stuff it into my duffel bag. The locker room has pretty much cleared out. Only Mangino and I are left, and the old custodian, who looks like he's worked here since Babe Ruth was a rookie.

"Wanna walk out together?" I ask Mangino.

He raises one eyebrow at me. At first, he grunts. Then he says, "Sure. Okay. Not quite ready yet."

He's still packing his stuff in his duffel bag, but I notice that he's folding everything neatly and in a specific order, unlike me.

"I'll wait for you, then."

"Yup. Yup. Yup."

That seems to be his mantra. Yup. Yup. Yup. He adjusts his cap to straighten it on his head and makes a move toward the door.

We walk to the parking lot in silence.

"How'd it feel pitching in the opening day game?" I ask.

"I didn't like it much. Too much pressure. But it's over."

"But you did fine, pitching out of a coupla jams," I say.

"But getting *into* those jams—that's what I don't like," he says. "I'd rather have Stevie catch for me than that Russ guy. He thinks he's better than anyone else."

"Russ? Really? I think he's great."

"*You* would," he says. "You like it when people tell you what to do. I'm my own man." He reaches way down into his duffel bag and pulls out a can. "Hey, wanna beer?"

A beer? A beer? I never drank a beer! I'm only 18, and my mother and father don't allow me to drink.

"Naw. I'm in training, you know..." and I laugh nervously.

"So…you're a goody two-shoes! I knew it!" and he lets out a belly laugh. "You've never even had a beer, have you?"

No, I haven't ever had a beer. I've never wanted one.

"Not lately. I've been in training, waiting to come here to play ball," I say.

"So tonight would be a good day for you to have a beer. Take this one. Go on, open it,"

he says.

I pop the top off the can and put it up to my lips. I hate the smell. He's looking at me with a real Yankee-fan smile, I think.

"Well? What are you waiting for? Don't you want a drink? I need a drink myself after the way I pitched today!"

I take a swig. Ugh. But I get it down, and the aftertaste is awful.

Bobby pulls a second can out of his duffel bag and pops the top. He begins to drink his own can, and he swigs large gulps without stopping. I am still on my first sip when he's just about finished the whole can.

I'd rather have a Coke or Pepsi any day, or lemonade.

Bobby reaches into the duffel and gets another beer. He pops the top and starts all over again. I continue to sip. Walk and sip. He drinks and gets silent again.

Why won't this guy talk? Who is he? Why is he here, if baseball stresses him out so much? He's good. He's moody and keeps to himself. And besides that, he's a Yankee fan. Maybe I spill out the details of my life too easily. That's who I am.

But he has the right to remain silent. And he does.

CHAPTER 21

The Season Ends

We didn't make the NY-Penn League playoffs.

We had a bunch of injuries in the infield, and Russ broke his index finger with a month left to go, leaving Skip to decide to platoon Johnny and Stevie behind the plate. Even though Bobby thought that Russ was a tyrant, it was obvious right away neither Johnny nor Stevie was ready to become our everyday catcher.

Jordan had his ups and downs as our closer. He blew 7 out of 17 attempted saves, and came close to giving up two more. Toward the end of the season, he looked wiped out, but he continued to work with Cesar on a one-on-one basis. Cesar told him to work on his conditioning during the off-season.

We had a scuffle over the center field position, when Jack Milkewicz took over from Tim Jakubowski after opening day, because Tim was suffering from plantar fasciitis. Jack was hitting the hell out of the ball for three weeks, when Tim was cleared to play again, and Jack felt he had earned himself the job for keeps. But when the trainer gave Tim the thumbs-up to return, Skip benched Jack in favor of Tim. Jack slammed his bat into the dugout bench, threw his glove at Finn when he tried to explain the situation, and spat at the ground when Tim walked past him.

Skip suspended Jack for three games, without pay. Jack told Skip he was going home.

"Fine," Skip said. "But I'll remind you, you have a contract, and you received a bonus for signing it. You gonna give that bonus back when you break that contract?"

Silenced, Jack sat on the bench between two rows of lockers. He stayed silent for the three days of his suspension. He didn't talk to anyone. But he didn't go home, either.

Guys got along best when we were on the road, when we were all staying in the same place, waiting for the bus at a hotel or at an away ballpark. We spent time together, grabbing a sandwich or a snack, and we drank beer together. No one seemed to be interested in hard liquor—whiskey or vodka, for example—or wine. Wine was for wusses.

Back to back, Bud and Bobby cleaned out their lockers on the final day of the season, engrossed in leaving nothing behind.

Bud removed all the big things—the extra shirts and rolled-up shorts, shoe laces, foot powder, jock strap, deodorant.

His duffel bag was almost full, and yet, he knew that something was missing. Pictures, he knew he had some pictures in there, somewhere. He looked down into one corner and found a folded-up newspaper.

It contained his grandmother's obituary from *The Atlanta Constitution*. He re-read it. *Maude Elwell Prescott, daughter of...survived by her only son, Cheslee, his wife, Rebecca, and her only grandson, Cameron "Bud" Prescott, a player in the minor league system of the Montreal Expos who will attend Vanderbilt University in Nashville in the fall.*

He sighed deeply, and felt tears coming to his eyes. *Don't let Mangino see me cry, Grandma.* He wiped his eyes with his sleeve and carefully placed the clipping in his pocket.

On the locker's floor, he saw a small peach-colored envelope with his name written in fancy handwriting. The return address on the back flap: Jennifer Murphy, Athens, Georgia. He pulled out the vellum note, which had the words "In Deepest Sympathy" written across a pinkish-yellow rose with a deep green stem. "My dear Bud, I am so sorry that you lost your lovely grandmother. She was indeed a special person to the entire community but especially to your family. I know this will leave a terrible hole in your heart. Thinking of you. Fondly, Jenny."

Fondly, Jenny. Hmmm...I never thought of her fondly, I don't think. I only thought about playing baseball and getting through school. That was very nice of her. Very nice. Fondly nice.

Bobby, on the other side, threw out three beer cans, six crumpled cheese-and-cracker wrappers, and a bunch of old napkins. He picked up a couple of old shirts and socks that needed serious hygiene therapy.

He fit what he could fit into his duffel bag, which already held his hat, cleats, glove, baseball pants, cup, and official team jersey. He'd saved a scorecard from one of the games he'd pitched, one Stevie caught.

Stevie is such a good, calm catcher. He and I could go places together. He doesn't ask questions, he just catches the ball. That's the way it should be. I know what I'm doing. Always have, always will. Thanks, Stevie.

But Bobby had never thanked Stevie personally. He didn't know how to thank people. No one ever thanked *him*. He watched Bud and Al thanking people, and he thought that made them weak.

He shoved the rest of his stuff into the duffel bag and zipped it, shutting out most of the odor, but not all.

Bud turned around and asked, "Are you ready to leave? We're the last two here."

"Yup, Yup, Yup," Bobby said. "Let's go."

"What do you have in that bag?" Bud asked. "It smells like Limburger cheese."

"What's that?" Bobby asked.

"Aged to perfection," Bud said. "Aged to perfection. Just like your old socks."

They walked out together. Bud knew enough not to put his arm around Bobby.

CHAPTER 22

Not Home Yet

Bobby had to take one Greyhound bus to Buffalo, and then another to the Port Authority in New York. Maybe he could get some sleep on the bus.

He had a couple of magazines in his duffel bag. *Sports Illustrated. Baseball Digest.* Maybe he'd buy an issue of *Playboy* when he got to Buffalo. Nah, people on the bus would be looking over his shoulder. Maybe he'd buy *Rolling Stone.* His reading skills weren't great, but he could follow the articles in *Rolling Stone.*

In the waiting room, his hard plastic seat rocked back and forth a little because it was missing a screw. *That's how I feel, most of the time—I've got a screw loose. I feel like my head's about to explode. Sometimes I just want to take a baseball bat and hit something when things don't go the way they should.*

An old woman who was all bundled up in a winter coat, with a wool hat on her head and a scarf around her neck, sat down next to him.

She asked, "Where are you goin'? I gotta go to Buffalo. I got a place in a senior apartment there. I came to Jamestown to see my sister. She's sick and in the nursing home. I'm Bernadette, by the way."

"I'm Bobby. Hi. I'm going to Buffalo and then back home, to New York," he replied. "Really, to Yonkers."

"Whad'dya doing in Jamestown? You got family here?"

"No, I been playing baseball with the Falcons," he answered.

"Oh...a *baseball* player! No wonder you're so handsome! Wait until I tell the other ladies in my apartment building that I sat next to a baseball player! They'll be so jealous!"

Bobby blushed. He was secretly pleased with the old lady's admiration. Maybe this was how Bud's grandmother had encouraged him, always telling

94

him how good he was. Bobby never had anyone telling him those things. His mother came to as many games as possible, but she never said things like this to him. His dad was absent, and he never knew his grandparents. *What would it have been like to know my grandparents?*

"Well, I'm just a low-level player for the Jamestown Falcons."

"Ah, but you WILL be famous, if you want to be," she said. "I know it! I just know it!" And she patted him on the shoulder.

Bobby flinched. He hated when people touched him, but he didn't say anything to her, the way he had said to his teammates and coaching staff.

"I guess you never know," he said. "My mother was upset because the Yankees didn't draft me, though."

"The Yankees? Oh, well, they could be kinda picky, don't you think?"

"I guess so," he said. "But my mother loves them, and they're the hometown team, you know."

"The hometown team...Yes. But you'll be fine. You just have to work at it. You'll see. Everything is worth it if you're willing to work at it, Bobby."

"If you say so," he said. "Yup. Yup. Yup."

The Buffalo bus pulled in.

"I guess this is our chariot," she said. "Let's get on board."

Bobby helped Bernadette up the stairs of the bus.

"Where do you want to sit?" he asked her.

"You pick," she replied. "You're the handsome one."

He smiled back at her, but only briefly. He picked the third row, and she took the one next to the window. She didn't remove her coat, scarf or mittens; she remained bundled up for the entire trip.

He got his magazines out of his duffel bag and put them in the pocket of the seat in front of his.

The bus driver started the engine and they were off. Once they'd reached Buffalo, the trip from Buffalo to New York City was about eight hours.

Bernadette was yakking away with stories about celebrities, and Bobby had tuned her out. She looked up at him and saw that he wasn't listening much, if at all.

"Am I boring you?" she asked.

"No," he replied, "I'm just a little tired."

"Oh....then I'll let you sleep. Good night."

She made a zipping motion across her mouth and abruptly stopped talking.

Silence.

He nodded off a few times but came back to his senses every time the bus hit a bump, or if Bernadette's sleepy head hit his shoulder. It didn't bother him, and that surprised him.

Both of them were half asleep, when they were jolted wide awake.

The bus lurched and went head first into a ditch on the right side of the road. Passengers sailed toward the front of the bus, shocked. Luggage flew, hitting people's heads, limbs and backs.

Bobby saw Bernadette thrown high toward the ceiling, then over the seat in front of them, landing near the driver's seat.

"BOBBY! BOBBY! BOBBY! WHERE ARE YOU?"

Shattered glass was everywhere. The driver was wedged between the door and the steps of the bus, unconscious.

The bus was stuck, front wheels first, in the ditch.

It was nearly pitch-black, and Bobby could only follow Bernadette's voice. He saw a small light from the back, a tiny flashlight on a keychain someone was waving.

He couldn't feel his legs. He tried to stand up by holding on to the top of one of the seats, but it didn't work. He felt something warm flowing down his face. He felt it with his finger: blood, coming from the top of his head. He found the cut over his left eye. He pressed his left hand against it to try to stop the bleeding, but it was no use.

Bernadette called out for him again, amidst the moans and screams of the other passengers.

"BOBBY! BOBBY! ARE YOU ALL RIGHT?"

"Bernadette! I'm still back here...I'm trying to get to you...Are you stuck?"

"I...I don't know...I haven't tried to move yet..."

"Stay put."

He didn't have the heart to tell her that he couldn't move his legs. He couldn't think clearly. He could smell diesel fumes and was worried that the bus could catch on fire.

A passing driver stopped and was banging on the door, yelling. "Is everyone okay?" Banging, banging, banging.

The driver started to wake up.

The man outside the bus was yelling to someone else.

"Get the tire iron out of the car! We need to pry this door open."

The bleeding over Bobby's eye had stopped. Bernadette was still on top of the steering wheel.

After a few tries, the men outside got the door open.

"Are you okay, man?" they asked the semi-conscious bus driver.

"Okay," he moaned in response.

The rescuer shouted, "Let's get as many people out of here as possible while we're waiting for help to get here."

They got the bus driver out and put him on the side of the road. After they got Bernadette out, they picked up two people who were in the aisle and were able to guide them out the door. Neither was hurt, as far as Bobby could tell, but it was very dark.

One of the men turned his car headlights toward the bus, to help get people out, but it also showed Bobby just how bad this accident was.

One by one, they carried people out to the grass by the side of the road. They had put Bernadette in their car, a Chevy sedan, because she told them she was cold, despite all those clothes she was wearing. Two children, maybe nine and ten, almost swam over the debris from the back to get out. Their mother had been hit on the head with some flying object, and she had temporarily lost consciousness. The kids were crying for her, but the helpers just told them to get out of the bus, and they did.

When they got to Bobby, he confessed that he couldn't move his legs. "Shit," said one of them, "I'm not sure if you're supposed to be forcibly moved if that's the case. Why the hell aren't the firemen here? We need them now!"

"I'm not sure what to do with you, man," the other man said. "We don't want to hurt you any more than you already are."

"Did you get everybody else out?" Bobby asked them.

"Just about. We think there may be one or two more way in the back, but we haven't been able to get up there yet," one replied.

"Go and get them and leave me until the bus is empty," Bobby said. "Maybe by then the firemen will be here."

"You sure?"

"Yup. Yup. Yup."

"Okay," one said, and they made their way to the back of the bus. It was like rock climbing, as they held on to the sides of seats and pulled themselves up the hill that was created when the nose of the bus dove into the ditch, throwing the back end up in the air.

They reached the two women who were left in the back. One was the mother of the two children. Dazed, she listened as they instructed her, "Just look at this debris on the floor, and we will help your kind of slide down it. One of us will be in front of you, the other behind. Just hold on."

One man in front held onto seats as the woman sat down, and the other man was behind. He grabbed her shirt as they slowly made their way atop the collection of stuff to the door, reuniting her with her children.

"Stay quiet. You've been hit by something, so take it easy."

They repeated their mountain-climbing-within-the-bus exercise, passing Bobby again, to get to the other woman who was clinging to a seat near the back of the bus, still very high up in the air.

They were relieved to hear sirens and see red lights flashing outside the bus.

As they reached the last woman, they discovered she was around 80 years old, the grandmother of the two children, the mother of the woman they had just evacuated.

"Should we leave her and let the real rescuers get her, or should we try to get her ourselves?" one asked the other.

"Let's see if we can get her, if she's comfortable trying what we did with her daughter," the other one responded.

She shook her head no, repeatedly.

A police car roared up to the bus, and two officers jumped out.

"One person, just tell us: Is there anyone else left inside?"

"Our grandma!" one of the boys cried out.

"And Bobby!" Bernadette screamed out of the side of the car.

"And the two guys who stopped to help!" someone from the back yelled.

"So that sounds like four people? Is that right?"

"Yes! Yes! Yes!"

"Okay, we have ambulances on the way. Let's see what we can do, partner."

One officer switched on his flashlight and pointed it into the bus. Bobby had to shield his eyes after having been in the dark for so long.

"In here!" one of the guys yelled.

"Okay," one of the officers said, "let's see—can we get the lady in the back out? Ma'am, please let these two fine gentlemen help you out. We will point the light for them, and they will help you. Will that work?"

It would.

The two men came out and spoke quietly to the officer. "I think we have one person who's really hurt," one guy said. "He says he can't move his legs. I don't know if that means anything, but we didn't want to move him. He's got to get out, though."

"Some of these other people out here may also find they have pretty bad injuries, once the adrenaline wears off," one officer said. "But okay, we'll go in. Smitty, bring the light."

"We got you," Officer Smitty said to Bobby.

They made their way to Bobby, holding on to the seat, stumbling over objects and suitcases. "So you can't move your legs?"

"No. I've stopped trying," Bobby said.

And then he began to cry.

"If I can't use my legs, I won't ever play baseball again…"

"Baseball? What do you mean?" Officer Smitty asked.

"I played this season with the Jamestown Falcons," he replied, sniffling.

"Well, crying ain't going to turn back time," the other officer said. "We'll get you on the ambulance as soon as it gets here."

They extracted Bobby from where he'd been wedged, between a seat, a piece of luggage and a typewriter. The typewriter probably hit his spine, Officer Smitty said.

Bobby winced as they removed the objects and set him down on the debris to slide him down toward the door.

More red lights. More sirens. The red lights were blinding Bobby. Two ambulances arrived.

Officer Smitty went to one of the ambulances, and spoke to the EMT.

"Get the guy we just took out. He can't feel his legs. Not a good situation. He's a pro ballplayer. Take him first."

"Okay," said the EMT, "but we have to evaluate everyone, you know."

"Yeah, I know," Officer Smitty said, "but this guy was the last one off. I think he should be the first one to get attention."

"Got it," the EMT said, as he ran the stretcher over to Bobby.

"What's your name?" he asked.

"Bobby—Robert Mangino, Jr."

CHAPTER 23

Bobby Needs Help

B ud gathered up the last of his things. He was headed home for a few weeks before setting out for his freshman year at Vanderbilt in Nashville.

He finished the season with a 10–2 record and a 1.93 ERA, and a .275 batting average. Skip and Cesar praised him for his success and told him he was making substantial progress.

He was imagining home without his grandmother, when the phone rang.

"Hello?"

"Bud?" a shaky voice said on the other end of the line.

"Bud? It's Bobby. Bobby Mangino..."

"Bobby? You sound so far away."

"I'm in the hospital. Our bus went off the road and I...I can't...I guess I can't move my legs."

"What? Where are you? What hospital?"

Another voice came on the phone. "This is a nurse at Chautauqua Memorial Hospital," she said. "To whom am I speaking?"

"Cameron Prescott," Bud responded.

"Are you related to Mr. Mangino?" she asked.

"No, but I played baseball with him in Jamestown. I think his mother lives in New York City," Bud responded.

"So he's calling you as next of kin?" she asked.

"I guess so," Bud said. "How far from Jamestown is Chautauqua?"

"Not far, but the roads are mostly winding back roads. Can you get here?"

"I don't have a car," Bud said, "but I'll find one. Can you tell him I'll get there as soon as possible?"

"Yes. He's been given some pain medication, so he's not entirely lucid. A lot of people were injured in this accident. We are fortunate that no one was killed in this one. The bus driver is in bad shape."

"Okay, thank you. Good bye."

Who has a car? Petrie? Jordan? No, I'll call Skip and Cesar. They'll know how to get there. Wow. Bobby. He can't move his legs.

He scrambled through his small bag until he found Skip's phone number. *And there's Cesar's. Call Skip first.*

Skip answered after three rings.

He said he'd take Bud to the hospital.

"But we need to call Cesar and bring him, too. Do you know if Bobby called his mother?" Skip asked.

"No, I don't, no, I'm not sure," Bud said. "The nurse said it was a bad accident and that they were lucky no one was killed.

"When can you pick me up? I can be ready in ten minutes," Bud added.

"Look, Bud, we'll be there in about 15 minutes. We know how to get to that hospital, so we should be all set. Bring your stuff with you, and we can try to get you to Buffalo from there so that you can start going home after we see Bobby. Got it?"

"Yes, I've got it, Skip," Bud said. "I'm almost completely packed. I just have a couple more things to stuff into the suitcase. I already said goodbye to my host family, and they're out for the night, anyway."

He hung up. He offered a silent prayer: *Dear God, please help Bobby, you who could help the lame walk and the blind to see…Look kindly on Bobby as he struggles to heal. And forgive him for his digressions from you. Amen.*

"Okay, be on the lookout for us. See you in a few."

Bud gathered the last few stray things he had to pack. He made sure he had his glove and the ball from his first win, as well as the one from the first home run he hit. Those were the important things, anyway; clothes could always be replaced, but those things could not.

Finally, he heard the engine of Skip's car in front of the house. Skip was driving his 1969 Chevy Impala, with Cesar in the front passenger seat.

"Sorry, Bud, I called 'shotgun' this time around," Cesar joked. and patted him on the shoulder. "Let's get *chore* stuff into the trunk."

Off they went, driving dark, winding roads. They passed the accident scene. The bus was still in the ditch, nose down, tail up, surrounded by yellow police tape. State police were marking off the accident site and taking flash photos of tire tracks on the pavement.

Around curves. Between farms. Up hills that made Bud's stomach sink. *It's a lot like rural Georgia here. Funny how a place that's so different can feel the same in the dark.*

Skip drove up the hospital entrance driveway and found parking. The three of them walked in together, stopping at the information desk to get Bobby's room number.

"But sir," he's in the intensive care unit. "Only family are allowed."

"We ARE family," Skip said. "We're going in."

"But sir...are you all...*related?*"

"Of course we are," Cesar said. "Can't *chew* see that we come from the same mother? Mother *béisbol!*"

The receptionist was speechless as the trio made its way to the ICU. When they arrived, they had to ring a bell. A nurse came to the door.

"We're here to see Bobby Mangino," the three of them said in unison.

"Are you all relatives of Mr. Mangino?" she asked.

"Yes, indeed we are," Skip replied.

"I spoke to someone on the phone..." Bud began.

"Are you Mr. Prescott?" the nurse asked.

"Yes, I am. Are you the one I spoke to earlier?"

"Yes, the very same. Now, I am going to give you all the same advice. He has taken pain medication and may not be very coherent. He will probably recognize you, but he's very sleepy. He's got a nasty bump over his eye, and it's kind of purple. I thought you should be warned about that," the nurse said.

"Okay," Cesar said. "We are warned."

The nurse led the trio to a small area where Bobby was hooked up to machines and monitors, all making noise, with ever-blinking lights of various colors.

She leaned in to Bobby and said softly, "Bobby, you have some visitors. I know you were expecting only one, but you have three."

Bobby opened one eye, then the other. He immediately recognized Bud.

"Skip? Cesar? How did you get here?"

"The better question is, son, how would Prescott get here if we didn't bring him?" Skip said.

"Coach, I can't feel my legs. I may be done."

"You gotta give it time," Skip said. "It's the end of the season. You'll probably be as good as new next year."

"I think I'm done, coach."

He started to cry.

This was the hard-nosed guy from Yonkers, the one who refused to make friends, and, by extension, made enemies, especially of others who were more talented than he was.

The one whose disdain got him into trouble with the managerial staff, the owners, the other players, and even the custodial staff.

And now here he was, crying like a baby.

CHAPTER 24

Eleven O'clock News

'm in my room at the Andersons' house for the last night. I have just about everything packed, prepared for when my mother and dad pick me up tomorrow afternoon. It's a long ride from the South Shore of Boston to this podunk town. I'll be glad to get back home, where there's some life in town. And I'm just a short ride away from Beantown, where I can go to see the Red Sox in person. And I can get good TV and radio stations.

Paul snagged a couple beers for me in my room tonight. He'll get me more out of the fridge if these are not enough. I'm just one of the guys when it comes to drinking beer now. I won't be 19 until next March, so I can't even buy my own beer in my own hometown, but it's tasting a hell of a lot better than it did on that night when I drank my first one with Bobby.

Mr. Anderson is down in the living room, watching the 11 o'clock news. He'll drift off to sleep. Mrs. Anderson will wake him up, and he'll shuffle off to bed.

My first season in the minor leagues was okay, but not what I expected. I thought I'd be a starter, not a reliever. I thought I'd get into more games than I did. I didn't think the competition would be as tough as it was.

At the end of the season, my ERA's just over 3, and I had a 2–1 record, which isn't bad for a middle reliever. I had a couple of bad outings, but then, the team didn't do all that well, either. We finished just a couple of games over .500 in the NY-Penn League, and the Williamsport Red Sox took the championship. I guess that bodes well for my Red Sox in the future, but I don't play for them.

I play for the Montreal Expos farm system.

I wonder if my luck would have been better with the Red Sox.

I'm in the middle of my first beer, when Mr. Anderson yells up to me.

"Jimmy! Jimmy! Get down here, now!"

Something must really be wrong.

"What? What's up, Mr. A.?"

"There was a bus accident—looks pretty bad—they have it on the news. I think one of your players was on that bus! Watch this!"

I sit down on the couch. I see a Greyhound bus with its nose in a ditch and its back end in the air, and the TV reporter talking about the people who were injured in the accident.

"We cannot confirm the extent of injuries of any of the passengers at this time, but we understand that one of the people who was among the most seriously injured is a player for the Jamestown Falcons, who was allegedly on his way home at the end of the season. We will have more details as they become available. Now back to you, Dave."

Oh, my God! I wonder who it is! Bud was going to take a bus to Buffalo tonight! I hope it wasn't him!

"They didn't give out his name before I got down here, did they, Mr. A.?"

"No, they didn't. They don't usually do that until they notify next of kin, Jimmy. Sorry."

"I just don't know who it could be. Lots of the guys have left already. One of my good friends was supposed to take that Buffalo bus tonight, but I thought he was leaving later."

"Give him a call," Mr. Anderson says, but I am already at the phone table, dialing Bud's number.

The phone rings. Eight times. Ten times. No answer.

CHAPTER 25

The Bus

Sergeant Moses from the New York State Police walks behind the bus, its back wheels up in the air and its nose stuck in a ditch. He shakes his head and mutters "mmm, mmm, MMM!" every few minutes as he looks for clues.

"Lucky only two people were seriously hurt," he says. "Wonder what that bus driver must be thinking now."

"What did you say, sergeant?" asks one of the investigators, from down in the ditch.

"Oh, nothin', just talking to myself," Moses replies. "Just ruminatin', that's all."

"Sergeant, I need to talk to you," Moses hears from behind.

"Who are you?" the sergeant asks.

"I'm Jimmy Bailey," I say. "I play for the Jamestown Falcons. I think my friend may have been on this bus."

"Oh, well, we just started the investigation, son. I can't release anything on anyone who was involved in the accident, but I can tell you that anyone who was injured was taken to Chautauqua Memorial Hospital. It's about four miles up the road."

"Thank you, sergeant. I borrowed a car, so I'll head up there. Wow, this is a mess, isn't it?"

"I'll tell you what, son, I wouldn't have wanted to have been on this bus," the sergeant replies. "We gotta figure out what happened."

I wave to the sergeant and run back to the Andersons' 1970 Ford Fairlane.

One mile, two miles, three miles, and then I see a sign for the hospital. I pull up and see Skip's '69 Impala, parked a few cars down.

"Oh, great," I think. Skip's here. "Oh, my God, it's gotta be Bud."

I stand up and run my hands through my hair, trying to steady myself enough to walk into the hospital and act like an adult.

This is life. I have little or no experience with life. These are the things my mother or dad would handle. Or even Debbie. But not me.

I walk through the hospital's automatic doors. It smells like bleach and antiseptic cleaner. Everything is white, white, white. Everyone who works here wears white—except the receptionist, who's wearing a pink coat with a round patch on the left shoulder. As I'm looking around, probably looking like a deer in the headlights, I see the receptionist looking up over her glasses and asking, in a very sweet voice, "May I help you, sir?"

"I...I...I am looking for my friend who was hurt in the bus accident," I stammer.

"Do you know his name?"

"Bud...er...Cameron Prescott."

"Let me look," she says, as she flips through a bunch of index cards. "Pres...Prescott...No, sir, we do not have a Prescott here. Are you sure that's the right name?"

"Well, I can see that my coach is here to visit someone," I say, "so it has to be someone on our team who was hurt in the bus..."

"Do you mean Bobby?" says a voice from the waiting room.

"Bobby?" I ask. "Bobby Who? And who are you?" and I turn around to see an old woman, wearing many layers of clothing and with a gash on her head.

"I'm Bernadette," she replies, "and I was on the bus with him. We were in the same row. He told me he was a player on the Falcons. He was on his way back to New York City, he said."

"Bobby Mangino? He was the one who was injured on the bus?"

"Yes, my Bobby," Bernadette replies. "He and I were talking about a bunch of things when, WHAM! the bus went into the ditch, and then all hell broke loose. I went flying over the seats and Bobby got wedged in. He can't move his legs."

"Can't move his legs?"

"Do you know his mother?" she asks. "Can you call her? She should know that he's in the hospital. I would want to know if it was my son."

"I don't know how to reach her," I say, "but I will ask the coach. He probably does. Let me think about this. Your name is Bernadette, right? Do you live in Jamestown?"

"No, but I was on my way to Buffalo, to see my sister. I plan to stay here until I hear more about Bobby. Can you find out and let me know? I'll be right here, that chair, over there."

"Um...okay...I'll go looking for the coach," I say. "Thank you, Bernadette, for waiting for Bobby. I'm sure he'll be happy to know you're still here."

I head off to the ICU.

I ring the bell. The door swings open. Out comes a nurse.

"Yes? May I help you? she asks, as she looks me up and down.

"Yes, ma'am," I say, "I am here because I think one of my teammates from the Falcons was hurt in a bus accident?"

"Are you his brother?" she asks.

"Well, in a way, ma'am, I guess I am," I respond.

"By that I mean, do you have the same mother?" she asks.

"Well, in a way, ma'am, I guess we do," I say.

The nurse finally gives in. "Okay, okay, come in. Three other guys are in there, so one of them will have to leave if you go in. No more than three visitors at a time. Do you understand?"

She motions for me to follow her, and I do.

The place smells weird, like blood-soaked bandages and cotton in the training room, like Mercurochrome and rubbing alcohol, like overused germicide and fresh, clean bed sheets. Monitors making strange beeps, all out of sync, all reporting signs of various stages of decline or improvement.

The nurse marches ahead of me into one of the rooms. "One of you will have to leave," she announces, "because there's someone else from your team who claims to be related to this guy, and he wants to see him. Strict orders are that only three people at a time can visit, even if they are 'related.' So which one of you is going to leave?"

Skip says, "I'll go."

Cesar protests, "No, I'll leave."

Bud chimes in, "No, let me leave. I'm the youngest."

"*Hijo, chew* may be the *chungest*, but he probably wants *chew* to stay here more than us old men," Cesar says. "So Skip and I will both leave for a while. We will come back soon, though."

Skip and Cesar come out of the room and see me. "Bos-tone?" Cesar says, as he's surprised to see me. "I thought *chew* had gone home!"

"No, my mother and dad are coming to pick me up tomorrow," I tell him.

Skip reaches out to shake my hand. "We're going to go downstairs to see if we can rustle up some coffee. You and Bud stay with Bobby for a while. We'll be back."

"Thanks, Skip. Thanks, Cesar."

I take a deep breath and walk in. I stay in the corner, since he and Bud are involved in a long conversation.

"See, Bud, I met this old woman in the waiting room at the bus station. Her name is Bernadette, and she was an odd person. I mean, it was hot, and she was all bundled up, in a thick coat and a scarf, and she was wearing thick gloves, too. She just started talking to me out of the blue.

"And we were sitting on the bus, just chugging along, and WHOMP! Off the road we went, and Bernadette went flying, all this stuff was airborne in the bus all around me."

He told Bud more details about the accident. He says Bernadette's concern for him made him cry.

CHAPTER 26

Going Home

I wasn't a scholar in high school, like Debbie was. Even my sister Donna was a good, solid student. My high school life revolved around baseball. If I was falling behind in one of my subjects, the coach would "have a conversation" with the teacher to see "what could be done" so I could at least get a C in that class, to stay on the baseball team.

For the most part, that worked. I got my diploma, graduated somewhere toward the lower end of my class, but I didn't really care.

Now I'm thinking, *should I have gone to the vocational school? Should I have learned to fix cars or make cabinets? How did Bud do both? School work and baseball work? How did he create his plan B?*

I'd basked in the limelight of being a baseball star. My dad didn't pressure me about the academic life because it wasn't important to him.

The Filly, on the other hand, never wanted me to play baseball, but then again, she couldn't stop the fast-moving locomotive that was my dad and me. I was the steam engine, and he was pumping coal into me.

My sisters made fun of my accomplishments on the ball field, but I knew they were proud of me. At home, they mocked me, but in public, they bragged about me to their friends and the local reporters who sat next to them at important games.

I hear a car pull up in front of 1048 Maryland Avenue. It's Dad and The Filly, arriving to pick me up and take me home for the rest of the summer, and then the winter. All my things are packed and waiting by the door.

"Mom! Dad!" I yell. "Come on in! I'm ready to go!"

The Filly gushes as she grabs me. "You look great—and tanned, too! Almost like you've been hanging at the beach!"

"Well, you know, playing ball..."

"Yes, playing ball," she repeats, rolling her eyes back, "...out on the field, standing around, wasting time..."

"Hey, Ma, can I talk to you?"

"Sure, baby, sure. Let's sit down," The Filly says. She walks over to the living room.

"Not on THAT one!" I say, as she's heading to Mr. Anderson's easy chair. "He'll know if you sit on it. He's got a second sense about it. It's weird. He says he knows from butt prints."

"How silly!" she says. "But okay."

"Ma, last night, Bobby, one of my teammates, was in a bad bus accident," I tell her.

"How awful! Is his mother here?"

"I dunno They were waiting for the doctor from Buffalo to come this morning," I explain. "But here's the thing. He can't move his legs. He has a spinal cord injury. They don't know if he'll ever be able to play ball again. I saw Bobby last night. He was the tough guy on the team, you know, the one who didn't get close to anyone, and he was crying. *Crying*, Ma. He's got nothin' now. Nothin'."

"Well, Jimmy, that's life," she says, "It's not pretty. We've seen it before. It's why I didn't want your father—or you—to play pro ball."

"So what would I do if it was me?" I ask. "Do I have a Plan B?"

"Plan B? You mean something you could fall back on if baseball doesn't work out?

"Yeah...Like Debbie could be a teacher, and Donna's going to nursing school. I could never do that. I couldn't get into college. I didn't do very well in school. It was all about baseball," I say.

"I know, I know," she nods. "It's never too late, you know. You can start to think about school. Go to Quincy Junior College, get some remedial courses done. Debbie could probably help you."

I interrupt her. "I don't want Debbie involved! If I'm going to do something like that, I want to do it on my own, and I don't want Debbie or Donna to know. Okay?"

"Okay, but what about Dad?"

"I'll talk to him about it myself," I say. "Don't tell him. I want to tell him myself."

"Well, I really don't want to see you working in that shipyard," she says. "It's breaking him in two."

"I know."

Dad comes in the front door right at that second and says, "Come on! I got everything loaded! You sure you got everything? Let's say good-bye to these good folks who have been taking care of you, and hit the road!"

Mr. Anderson is at work, but Mrs. Anderson is home. I go and pull her out of the kitchen, reach out and give her a hug. She has tears in her eyes as we say goodbye.

CHAPTER 27

Mrs. Mangino Arrives

B obby had nodded off in the hospital's ICU, thanks to his pain meds. He woke up when a tall, thin doctor, about 50 years old, rushed into the room, his unbuttoned white coat flapping as he walked, followed by two other doctors and two medical students. *He has a big group with him? What does that mean?*

"Mr. Mangino? I'm Dr. Levinson. I just got here from Buffalo. I'm the head of neurosurgery at the School of Medicine." He reached out his hand to shake Bobby's. Bobby nodded at him.

"I see you're probably dealing with the pain medication we gave you," Dr. Levinson said. "That's okay. We need to talk about your condition."

Bobby saw that the nurse who had kicked Skip and Cesar out earlier was standing in the doorway.

"Close the door, will you, please, nurse?" Dr. Levinson said.

"Okay, then, Bobby...We've discovered that you severed your spinal cord in the lumbar region—that is, in your lower back. That is why you have lost control of your legs. You probably have also lost control of your bladder and bowels.

"I want to take you to the hospital at the medical school so we can get a physiatrist to evaluate your condition."

"I don't need a shrink!" Bobby yelled. "I am perfectly capable..."

"I didn't say a *psychiatrist*, Bobby, I said a *physiatrist*. That's a doctor who specializes in physical medicine and rehabilitation. Lots of sports stars see physiatrists when they are injured, and I would like you to work with the guy we have at our hospital. He's very talented, and I believe he might be able to help you."

"Help me? Help me get my legs back so that I can play ball again?"

"I can't make any promises, Bobby, but I think he's our best shot. We need to get you stabilized and get you ready to travel. Are you okay with this?"

Before he could speak another word, Bobby's mother came flying into the room, almost knocking over the nurse.

"OH, MY GOD, BOBBY! What have they done to you? Get out of my way, Mr. White Coat! Don't touch my Bobby!"

She flung herself on top of Bobby, and he could barely breathe.

"Ma, get off me! I need to hear what this guy has to say."

"You'll do no such thing! We are taking you to New York City, where all the best doctors in the world are!"

Bobby looked up and saw Bud was also in the room. "Has she been this hysterical since you picked her up?"

"As you might say, Bobby, yup, yup, yup," Bud replied. "She's been pretty upset."

Bernadette, who was with them, sheepishly walked in, looking at the floor.

"Bobby, I've been wanting to see you since that bus…"

"Bernadette, you don't have to be shy. Ma, I want you to meet my friend, Bernadette! Bernadette, this is my mother, Angie—Angela—Mangino."

"What is going on here?" Mrs. Mangino asked.

Dr. Levinson and Mrs. Mangino proceeded to have what Bud called "a lively conversation" for about half an hour. Bud left the room to call Skip, who said he would come back and pick up Bud so that he could get the rest of his stuff and finally go home himself.

Bud went back to the ICU to find Dr. Levinson and Mrs. Mangino both gone. Bernadette was still there, and she and Bobby were speaking quietly.

"Excuse me for a second," Bud said. "I just want to say that I'll be leaving soon. Bobby, please let me know how things are going." He reached into his wallet and pulled out a fragment of paper. He wrote down his home phone number and gave it to Bobby.

"I will let you know," Bobby said. "Thanks, man, for coming to help me."

"Yeah, no worries. No one knows why things happen the way they do, when they do. Besides," he added, "you never would have met your grandmother if it hadn't been for the bus station, right?"

"You're so right, man. I hereby adopt her as my grandmother, right here and now."

Bobby looked over at Bernadette, and they exchanged big-toothed smiles.

Bored at Home

'm back home, sitting on my twin bed, and I have nothing to do. Zilch. Zero.

The phone rings. It's Bud. "Jimmy? Can you talk for a minute?"

"Gotta give you the update on Bobby."

"Where is he, Bud?"

"He's in the hospital in Buffalo—the medical school, seeing some specialist there. I haven't heard any more details than that. I'm waiting to hear back from Skip and Cesar. They're in contact with the medical team and his mother. That's about all I know."

"Wow. Wow. What else can you say?"

"I don't know. I guess you never know what to say. Or think." Bud's voice trails off a little. He pauses for what seems to be a long time.

"They say something really bad happened to his spinal cord. He may never walk again. May never play baseball, for sure."

I need a beer. I need a drink. This is how I've learned to comfort myself this summer.

"Will you let me know if you hear anything Bud? I mean, you're getting ready to go off to college, right?

"Call me when you get to school so I have your number, okay?"

I feel like I'm whining. I'm starting to feel a little desperate for a beer.

"Sure, Jimmy, sure. Hope things are going okay at home," Bud says.

How does he always know the right things to say?

"I'm just hangin' out with my sisters," I reply. "They're pretty cool."

"Okay. I'll keep in touch."

His southern drawl is soothing to me. Like a long pull on a cold beer, on a hot day.

"Great, Bud. Have fun at college."

What would I do if I couldn't walk anymore? I think I'd just fall into a heap on the sidewalk and want to shrivel up and die. Or ask someone to put me out of my misery. I wonder if Bobby feels that way.

I want to talk to Debbie and Donna about this, but neither of them is in the mood. They're both getting ready for college. It will be Debbie's first year of graduate school and Donna's first year of nursing school. Donna's going away to the University of Georgia for nursing school.

Why the hell can't she stay closer to home? Hey, isn't that where Bud is from?

Debbie is getting a master's degree in urban planning. What the hell is *that*, anyway, urban planning?

I need a beer. In fact, maybe I need a six-pack. Or two.

How will I get beer, now that my "connection"—Paul Anderson—is nine hours away? Who will be my Paul now that I'm home? I gotta find someone. I could buy if I were still in New York, but the drinking age here in the good old Commonwealth of Massachusetts is still 21.

I knock on Debbie's door.

"Hey, sis, what're you doing?"

"Just packing my stuff," she says. "I'm going to Harvard, but I don't want to live at home. I'm getting an apartment in Cambridge with a couple of my friends. I'll be the only one in grad school. The other two are working. You remember my friend who wanted to be the sportswriter?"

"Yeah. She used to write letters to the editor about baseball and the Red Sox."

"She's one of my roommates. We got an apartment on Agassiz Street, kind of near Radcliffe College. She had to drop out of school because her parents ran out of money. She's working as a secretary at MIT."

"Do you think you'll like going to school?"

"It'll be all right. I know I can make a lot more money if I get a master's degree. Maybe I'll go for a doctorate after that."

"Why do you need so much school?" I ask.

"It's all about the connections and the money you can make," she says. "And I really do learn a lot."

"Well anyway, sis, do you think maybe you could score me some beer?"

"Beer? Since when do you drink beer?"

"Since I went on the road with the team. We all drank a coupla beers every night when we were on the road."

"Sure, I can get you a couple of beers, but you'd can't let dad catch you."

"Okay. I can go down to the beach and drink. Or I can go out in the backyard, way up in the woods. Do you need money?"

"No, I'll head out to the packie and get it for you. Just this once. You know?"

"Yeah, I know."

She heads downstairs and grabs her keys.

"I'm going to do an errand," she tells The Filly.

"Okay, dear, drive carefully."

CHAPTER 29

Bobby's Ride to Buffalo

An orderly rolled a gurney into Bobby's ICU room.

"Time to get this show on the road," he said. "I'll be driving this train!"

Bobby was worried about what was going to happen next. Dr. Levinson was optimistic, but he wasn't.

His vision was foggy, and he didn't know if it was the pain medicine or if his brain had actually become cloudy. The chaos that followed the accident only intensified after his mother came and tried to bully Bernadette.

He couldn't make sense of anything. He just wanted to feel his toes again. He wanted to stand up on his own. He wanted to do something simple, like go to the bathroom without help.

Instead, he looked down and saw a plastic bag filled with his urine—and he didn't know how it got there. He had no idea how the water he drank converted from his mouth to the stomach to the kidneys to the bladder, but the nurse told him he must be drinking enough, because his urine was what she called "a nice, pale yellow."

Oh, great, for one time in my life, I'm doing something right. I'm drinking enough water to keep my urine pale. Whoopie. So how much would I get in my paycheck for producing "nice, pale, yellow" urine?

The orderly tapped him on the shoulder and said, "Hey, buddy, we're going to move you onto the gurney now. It's your chariot that will take you to the ambulance."

He saw the nurse he liked on one side and the orderly on the other.

"Am I covered up? I mean, I wouldn't want anyone to see my legs that I can't feel on the way down the hall."

"Yes, Bobby, you're covered up," the nurse replied. "Do you think I want to share you with anyone else in this hospital?"

He smiled at the thought that the nurse was flirting with him. No one ever did that before. At least, not someone as nice and cute as she was.

Bobby looked at the ceiling as they were going down the hallway. Ceiling tiles, some straight, some crooked, and some lights were stronger than others, went by, almost as if he were riding on the New York subway, but without the constant noise.

They came to an elevator, and somebody pushed the down button. As the doors opened, Joe the orderly decided to back into the elevator, so he made a beeping sound, as if he were a truck and needed to beep when he backed up.

When they got to the front door, Bobby saw his mother and Bernadette, and Skip and Cesar.

His mother came over to the gurney and said, "Bobby, Bobby, these nice men are going to drive me and Bernadette to Buffalo. We'll get there as soon as we can."

Bernadette came over as well. She leaned in and said quietly, "You'll be fine. Just listen to what they tell you, and you'll be fine. Take a pain pill if you need to. My sister's going to meet us at the hospital, too."

The nurse put one hand on the gurney and said to him, "Bobby, I know you're worried. But Dr. Levinson's one of the best. And by the way, my name is Maureen. I'll be thinking of you."

"Thank you, Maureen. But guess what? I already knew your name."

As the EMTs collapsed the gurney and eased it into the back of the ambulance, Cesar called out to him. "*Chew* know what to do, Man-GEE-no! *Yust* get rolling, okay?"

"Okay, Cesar. And Skip? I got it."

As the EMTs closed the ambulance's back doors, they all waved in unison.

When the ambulance drove away, Mrs. Mangino broke down.

"He'll never walk again, will he?"

"Maybe not, Mrs. Mangino," Maureen said. "But he's going to need you to be strong now more than ever."

"Oh, my God!" she said, continuing to scream, "My Bobby! My Bobby!"

No wonder he was looking for a grandmother, Bernadette thought. *Someone needs to be stable in this family. His mother is kinda crazy. I'm the Rock of Gibralter next to this one here.*

CHAPTER 30

Weymouth, in the Woods

It's a nice night, and Debbie returned with a six pack of beer. It's not the kind that Paul used to buy for me in Jamestown, but it will do.

"Thanks, sis, I owe you one," I tell her.

"Hey, you owe me a lot more than that," she says, as she throws her keys back into her pocketbook. "I've gotta go finish getting my stuff together."

I head for the front door. My dad is out in the back, in the shed. He won't see me leave. If I walk about a block from here, there's a patch of woods where I can sit alone and just have a couple of these beers. Yeah. That's a plan.

Debbie had the guys at the packie put the beer in a brown paper bag. What a concept! Putting beer in a brown paper bag. She's a genius.

I walk down the street and wave to a couple of neighbors. "Hi, Mrs. Morrissey, how're you doing?"

"Fine, Jimmy! Nice to see you home."

"Thank you. Say hi to Dougie for me."

"He's in the Army now, in Vietnam," she says. "You should write him a letter."

"Oh, right, I'll get his address from you tomorrow."

"That would be so nice, Jimmy. He would love to hear from you and hear about your baseball playing. He always loved to play baseball with you."

"Thanks, Mrs. Morrissey. See you later."

Dougie in Vietnam? What the hell? I got out of the Army because I had a high draft lottery number. Did he volunteer? Did he get drafted? I'm trying to picture Dougie in an Army uniform, in the jungle, with a real gun. We used to play army when we were young. My dad would make me stop when he got home from work to throw with him. Dougie. In the Army. Wow.

I am right near the woods where I want to drink my beer. Everyone comes here to drink, and sometimes to smoke weed. I tried that a couple of times with Paul, but I really prefer beer.

I sit down under a tall maple tree. I pop the top on the first can, and take a long gulp, letting out a long, "AHHHH!" It tastes so good. I craved a drink the entire drive home from Jamestown. As I sit, I dig my heels into the dirt, almost like the way I do when I am pitching. I find a little stick and draw a line. This will be my pitching rubber, I decide, and if I want to throw something, I will start here. And keep drinking.

I wonder how Bobby is doing. I wonder if Bud ever made it home. I wish I were going to college in a few weeks. Maybe I can go visit Donna when she's in nursing school down there where Bud is from, sometime when he's on school break. Maybe I could go and meet Bud's mother and father, and see that big house that his grandmother had. I should go to visit Bobby. Where is he? Is he in Jamestown or in New York City? I hate New York City.

I open my second can of beer. I put the empty in the brown paper bag.

What did management think of my season? Is a 3.19 ERA good enough? Will they promote me to Double-A? I know Bud will go, and probably Russ and John Jordan. But who else? Joey? But how is Bobby? Where is he? Who is taking care of him? Will he walk again? Will he play ball again? Oh, my God! How can your life change that fast? What is my Plan B?

As I open can number three, I hear crunching footsteps. If it's the cops, Debbie's going to be in trouble for buying me this beer. I stand up—a little wobbly.

It's two guys I knew in high school, Terry Bingham and Eddie O'Donnell. I'm not sure they recognize me. Eddie's carrying a brown paper bag, too.

"Terry? Eddie?"

"Who's there?" Terry asks.

"It's me...Jimmy..."

"Jimmy? The baseball player?"

"Yep."

"Hey, man, how're doing? When did you get home?" Eddie asks.

"Just yesterday. I was playing ball in Jamestown, New York. I decided to come out here to clear my head, get out of the house for a while."

"We decided to come out here to drink!" Eddie says, with conviction. "Wanna beer?"

"That's okay, I have one of my own," I say, raising my can to them.

"You drink?" Terry asks. "Never knew you to do that in high school. You were always such a goody two-shoes."

"Yeah, I guess so," I say, "but things change, people make other choices."

"So you learned how to drink when you got into baseball? Is that what happened?"

"Kinda," I say.

CHAPTER 31

Dad at Home

As I walk up the steps of our house, I'm feeling the beers. I have the three empties in the brown bag, along with the three full cans from the six pack. I walk back down the steps to ditch this stash. But where? Behind the shed? Behind the doghouse? In the old car dad is working to restore?

I decide on the doghouse, because we haven't had a dog for about 10 years, when my dog Pepe died after getting hit by a car. Thinking of Pepe brings tears to my eyes, and soon they're full-blown tears. I can't stop. Is it the beer?

Pepe! I loved you so much! You were the only thing in my life that never put any pressure on me! I miss you, old pal.

And the tears keep flowing as I carefully hide the beer behind Pepe's former hideaway. Pepe loved to go in there and put his treasures out of sight. If Pepe were here, would he be okay with my illegal brew in his special place? I convince myself that he'd just put his head on my leg and look up at me with those soulful eyes of his while I was drinking, as if to say, *Well, if that's what makes you happy.*

But it didn't make me happy. It was making me cry about a dog who'd been gone since I was in sixth grade.

What the hell?

I got myself together enough to tackle the stairs again. I open the screen door, and there he was, as big as life: Dad, sitting in his favorite chair, reading the newspaper.

"Hey, Jimmy, where've you been? I was looking for you."

"I was out," I say, like a stupid teenager would. "I ran into a couple of my old friends from high school."

"Who?"

"Terry and Eddie. Do you remember them?"

"Those bums? You hung around with them? They're nothing but bums! They don't have jobs, they're going nowhere. Don't let them suck you in, son," Dad warns.

"We were just talking about high school, Dad," I reassure him.

He gets up out of the chair and comes over to me. "You've been drinking! I can smell it! Those bums tried to get you drunk!"

"No, Dad, they were just being hospitable when they offered me a beer," I say.

"A beer? You're supposed to be in training! How do you expect to make it to the majors if you don't take care of yourself?"

"I don't see any harm in a beer or two every now and then," I protest.

"Except for the fact that you could be arrested for being an underage drinker!"

He pulls me up to his face and says, "Look at this face! Look at these hands! Do you want to have hands like this? Do you want wrinkles and lines in your face when you're my age? I taught you everything so you don't have to do manual labor, like I do. Do you understand?"

Pepe, Pepe, Pepe!

"Yeah, Dad...I..."

"You might as well go tomorrow and fill out an application at the shipyard. Maybe they'd hire you on the spot because your old man has a reputation for having a good work ethic. Do you have a work ethic? At all? You learned anything at all from me?"

I learned so much from you, Dad, but the biggest thing I learned is that I can't fail, because if I do, I'm not failing myself, I'm failing you.

"What do you want me to say?" I ask.

"What do I want you to *say*? How about what do I want you to *do*? I want you to work hard so that you'll go places—places I never had the chance to. Don't you want that?"

"I'm not sure I'm ready for that."

"Of course you're not ready. That's what the minor leagues are for—to get you ready! That's why you climb up the ladder and aren't just plunked into major league ball."

I'm waiting for the rest of the lecture: I gave up my chances for your mother, and that means for you and your sisters, too, so I am counting on you not to blow this. You've got it all. Don't let it go. How could you?

But the rest of the lecture doesn't come. Instead, he throws the newspaper down on the chair and stomps up the stairs. "Mary, I'm going to bed!"

I could use the soulful eyes of a dog right now. I could use a wagging tail, a lick on my hand to tell me everything is all right. But everything isn't all right.

CHAPTER 32

Buffalo Medical School

Bobby leaned up on one elbow. He was getting tired of this. Sure, they put him in a wheelchair every now and then, and he could go up and down the hallway, but what did he see? He saw the hospital from more and more angles. People in white coats. He was getting sick on that antiseptic smell, too. The food here was terrible.

His mother had to go home to Yonkers. She couldn't leave his brother Charlie alone anymore. The Manginos had no other relatives they could turn to, including Bobby's deadbeat dad.

At least Bernadette came to visit every now and then. She and her sister, who lived in Clarence, baked him brownies or cookies and came to dote on him every couple of days. Sometimes they brought him an edible dinner.

He liked it when they came. He had adopted them as his relatives. He continued to imagine that Bernadette was his long-lost grandmother He discovered Bernadette was a widow, with no children of her own. She had been a secretary in the Buffalo branch office of the New York State Department of Health for 30 years, and she retired with a nice pension. She took bus trips to visit her siblings now.

Bobby wanted to ask Bernadette how her husband died, but he didn't know the right words to use, ones that wouldn't hurt her feelings. She finally told him her husband had a heart attack on one bitter cold January day.

"Bobby, he was only 48 years old, only 48!" Bernadette added. "He had so much more life in him…I don't know why he was taken from me so early on…I just loved him so… I still hope to see him come home. I guess you never get over these things.

"Ah, let's not talk about this anymore," she said. "How about getting into your chair and we'll pop some wheelies! We can go down the hall and see what we can see. What'dya say?"

"Okay, we need to call the nurse to get me out of this bed and into the chair," he said, as he grabbed and pushed the call button.

A few minutes passed, and then the nurse came in and asked what he needed.

"I want to get up in the wheelchair," he said. "My chauffeur here wants to take me for a spin down the hallway."

Bernadette pushed him down the hallway, half skipping, half walking, to the TV room. He had a TV in his room, but it was tiny, so it was difficult for him to see a ball or a puck while he was lying in his bed. It was much better, anyway, if he was sitting up, and he was just getting to the point where he could get himself into a sitting position in his bed.

The accident had left him a paraplegic.

Paraplegic.

His spinal cord had been severed in the lumbar region, and the chance of his ever walking again was just about slim and none. Dr. Levinson told him that it was one of the worst things he's ever had to tell anyone.

"I just don't know what to say," Bobby remembered Dr. Levinson telling him. "I wish I knew of a miracle cure. I wish I could say that I knew someone—anyone in the world—I could send you to who could make it better, but I don't. I will keep searching."

Searching. Searching. That's what we're all doing. We're searching. And I can't even go home because I can't get this wheelchair or this broken body up umpteen flights of stairs. My mind works and my body doesn't any more. The only thing I know how to do is play baseball, and now that's over. What am I supposed to do? Where am I supposed to go?

The nurses were nice enough here. Sometimes they'd bring him treats and magazines, but he really didn't want to stay in a hospital much longer. Sure, it was nice getting visits from Bernadette and sometimes her sister, but he never heard from anyone from his team. They had scattered to the winds, all going home to whatever was waiting for them.

Even the coaching staff. Cesar was in the Dominican, working with some young kids he thought might make good prospects. "*Chew* wouldn't believe how poor they are, Man-GEE-no. They don't even have no gloves. They catch balls with pieces of cardboard on their hands. They make balls out of old socks they put together. They're dressed in rags. Rags! But they love the game. I should take *chew* with me some day. *Chew* would like to see how blue the water is there. But poverty—*chew* ain't never seen nothing like it. Never."

Skip was coaching fall ball in Arizona. He would be working with a bunch of Double-A guys from the Montreal system, mostly on strategy and other drills. Mick the Stick would be there to work with them on hitting as well. Arizona sounded good to Bobby, especially when compared with Buffalo. He had no idea what to expect of what winter could bring to the city, specifically because of the rumors nurses had told him about all that lake-effect snow that could come off Lake Erie.

A few days later, a social worker came into his room and told him that she was working to get him a new place to live. Little did he know that she was talking about a nursing home. He knew he wasn't ready to live on his own, but he didn't want to be surrounded by old people, either.

She told him about Brothers of Mercy in Clarence, the same town where Bernadette's sister lived. He completely freaked out, saying, "I can't live with a bunch of old people! I know what nursing homes smell like! I'm not leaving here!"

"Hold on, Bobby," she said. "Let me tell you about Brothers of Mercy. They have a young adult unit, and it's completely different from some of the places you may have heard about. Part of the reason it's taken me this long to find you a spot is that I didn't *want* you to go to a place that was only for elderly people. This young adult unit has several other people—guys, mostly—who are in a situation like yours."

"Really? I didn't know such a thing existed."

"Well, it does, and you're not alone. I'll take you on a 'field trip' out there tomorrow, and you can meet some of the people who work there and see the place."

Bobby thought for a few minutes. He looked out the window. He looked down at his legs—*useless things, they are*, he thought. *They used to help me propel a ball, run bases, and now look at them! Nothing more than two logs in a bed.*

Finally, he looked back at the social worker and said, "Okay. Field trip. Tomorrow. Yup. Yup. Yup."

He was surprised when he heard himself say those three "yups" in a row. He hadn't said that for a while. Maybe some of his old self was returning. He needed to get some of his old sass back, but he also needed to figure out where he was going.

What was it that Bud and old Bos-tone called it?

Plan B?

He needed one now. Desperately.

CHAPTER 33

Get a Job

After about a month of lounging around the house all day then sneaking out at night to go drinking with Terry and Eddie in the woods, I'm bored. I've even stopped working out—what little I did.

I sleep late every day, and The Filly makes me breakfast, no matter what time I get up. She looks adoringly across the table at me as I eat, telling me how much I look like Dad when he was my age.

"You're so handsome!" she says. "That's why I fell for him, you know. He was so handsome, like a movie star."

"Oh, Ma, cut it out!" I say. "I'm not Dad!"

"No, but you are handsome, just like he was, and so talented!" The Filly says. "Jimmy, he works so hard, and he is so proud of you! He just loves you so, but he doesn't know how to show it."

"Ma, I want to get a job. Where can I get a job around here?"

"Let me think…Building 19 is just over the bridge in Hingham. They might have openings. There's always Stop & Shop, or Mister Donut. You could check out the Weymouth Marina, but I don't know if they have people working there over the winter. And Weymouth Volkswagen. They're pretty close by," she says.

"I think I'll go out and try to put in some applications," I reply.

"Good luck, dear," she says. "Don't forget to finish your breakfast." I'm beginning to understand why Dad fell in love with *her* those many years ago. Not only is she still beautiful, but she's kind and caring. She's like that with my friends and those of my sisters, too.

But there must have been something extraordinarily special about her that made him give up baseball for her.

Something children can't see. Something inexplicable that only becomes evident when they grow up and have their own spouse, children, mortgages and responsibilities, their own bills to pay.

It's time to find a job.

CHAPTER 34

Brothers of Mercy

The social worker wheeled Bobby down the hallway and out to the front circle where she had parked the hospital's van. One of the orderlies came with them and helped get Bobby into the passenger seat, then folded up the wheelchair and put it in the back of the van.

Bobby was nervous. This was the first time he'd been upright in a vehicle since the bus accident. His mind swirled as he thought for a second about the last time he had moving wheels under him. He fumbled for the seat belt. He began to sweat, even though it was not very warm inside the van. He wiped the sweat off his face with the sleeve of his shirt. He hoped the ride to Clarence was short.

When they pulled up to the horseshoe-shaped driveway of Brothers of Mercy, the social worker went inside for a minute and came out with someone to help get Bobby out of his seat and into the wheelchair.

It was a male nursing assistant, who was about as big as Bobby himself, and he introduced himself to Bobby.

"Hi, I'm Hank, and I'll be your driver today!" he said, smiling, and then added, "but first we have to get you out of your stagecoach."

He then looked at Bobby and asked for his name.

"Bobby," he replied. "Bobby Mangino."

"Well, Bobby Man-GEE-no," We're going to have a good time today!" Hank assured him.

Bobby found it funny that Hank said his name like Cesar did.

They walked down the corridor filled with paintings by the residents. Bobby didn't detect any strange "nursing home-type" smells while they were traveling down the hallway.

They arrived at a unit with a sign over the door: "Faith, Friends, Family." Hank wheeled Bobby in.

Just like the social worker had told him, everyone was under the age of 40. Most were between 20–25, and everyone was in a wheelchair. A couple of those chairs were motorized, and their occupants controlled them with joysticks to allow them to make left and right turns or go forward or backward.

Bobby saw some residents who were involved in art class, while some were playing board games and a couple were playing ping-pong while sitting in their wheelchairs. Five of them had gathered around the television and were cheering while some contestant was winning "The Price is Right."

Hank wheeled Bobby over into a semi-quiet corner. Then he brought two residents over to speak with Bobby.

"Bobby, this is Jonesy—and this is Mark. They can answer any questions you might have about living here," Hank said.

Both Jonesy and Mark leaned over in their wheelchairs and shook hands with Bobby. "Nice to meet you," each said.

"You thinking about coming to live here?" Jonesy asked.

"Yeah, I'm getting the grand tour," Bobby said.

"Well, it's not so bad. They're pretty good to us here. They even give us good food. You can't say that everywhere," Mark said. "I was at another place, and I was the only young person in the place. It was pretty bad. They only gave me pureed food. You've never *lived* until you've had pureed roast beef!"

They all laughed.

"I can only imagine," Bobby said. "Or maybe not."

"It does take a while getting used to it, though," Jonesy said. "It's not like living at home, not by a long shot."

"Well, I've been living in the hospital at the medical school in Buffalo," Bobby said, "and I guess they need to kick me out. I don't have anyone my own age on the floor. This could be an improvement."

"Could be," Jonesy said.

Hank came over and said, "Hey, break it up, you guys! You're going to scare him away!"

The three of them wheeled off together to look at the rest of the unit, looking at the art room, the physical therapy area, the dining room, and other areas of interest.

After they'd gone, the social worker asked Hank, "Do you think he might try it?"

"Those guys have the same injury he has," Hank replied. "One came from a car wreck, too—Jonesy. This is the best anyone can do in this part of New York. If he wants to go to Saratoga, there's a place with a young adult unit there, too. There may be something in New York City, but it's so hard to get in there."

"He's from New York City—Yonkers, actually—so I'm sure he'd rather be going there, but if there's a long waiting list…"

"Trust me, if he wanted to go to the place in New York City, it would probably take him two, maybe three years," Hank said. "Besides, isn't the goal to get him to the point where he could learn to take care of himself? We got the guy whose room he'd be taking out of here a couple of days ago because he got an accessible apartment and can take care of himself now, with a little home care assistance. Isn't that what you think is best for him, too?"

"That's exactly right," the social worker said. "And I plan to explain that to him on the way back to the hospital."

"Try prying him away from these guys," Hank said. "They look like they're having a good time."

"Yes, this is the most life I've seen in him since I first met him."

CHAPTER 35

Vanderbilt

Bud packed his car as it sat in Lindenwood's horseshoe-shaped driveway.

He put the footlocker in the back seat and his baseball gear in the trunk. Beyond that, he figured, he didn't need anything else, although his mother fussed with him over taking a couple of sets of sheets and a bedspread, along with towels and a little cloth bag she made for him to put his shaving cream and razor in.

"Mama," he protested, "this is kind of 'girlie,' you know, this cloth bag. I think I want to get a leather shaving kit instead. I think I'll stop somewhere along the road and find one."

"Oh, *Cameron*," she said, using his full first name, which she so rarely did, "would you insult your mama that way? I mean, I made it just for you… It'll make you think of your mother when you're so far away from home."

She had embroidered his initials on the handle.

"Really, Mama? Really?" He rolled his eyes.

He kept putting things into the car until he was ready to roll. The August sun beat down on his head, and he felt sweat rolling down his back.

Funny, I'm hardly moving, but I'm sweating. I could be throwing a ball and it would feel good. Just standing here, perspiring without exerting myself, is a waste. I want to throw a ball. I need to throw a ball.

He could feel his feet moving back and forth, almost as if he were getting ready to position himself on the pitching rubber. He looked up, half expecting to see Russ, 60 feet, six inches away from him, crouched down, giving him a signal about what to throw.

Instead, he saw the four white Doric columns of Lindenwood, approximately the same distance away, standing straight and strong, holding up the legacy of his entire family, with the torrid Georgia sun beating down on the roof.

I am not playing baseball today. I am leaving for college. College. Vanderbilt University. Nashville, Tennessee. Not Georgia. Leaving home. By myself. Not on a team. Yet.

Rebecca approached him and said, "You'd better get going, Bud. You have a long drive ahead of you. I don't want you to go, but the longer you delay, the harder it gets for me."

"Yes, Mama, I know, I know."

He reached down and gave her one more hug and then turned toward his car. The chrome was hot when he touched it, so he quickly grabbed the handle and pushed the button, opening the door. He rolled down the window to let in some air.

His mother handed him a hundred dollars through the window.

"Just a little something to carry you through, in case you need something when you're on the road," she said.

"You're always taking care of me," he said, as he smiled back at her, his face squinting against the sun.

She saw his smile—It swallowed up his face and was at least as bright as the sun itself. It always had been, since he was an infant. She remembered his baby face, without teeth, then with teeth, and now, here he was, her only child, her son, all grown up and getting ready to leave for college.

She didn't want him to see her cry. He knew she would, though. He was having a difficult time not crying himself, even though he knew he should be strong. He didn't want her to know that he was scared—afraid he might fail as a college student, fail his parents' expectations, and most of all, fail his grandmother. As he sat in the driver's seat, ready to turn the key in the ignition, he wasn't so sure of himself.

She leaned in one more time and gave him a kiss on the cheek. "You'll be fine, my baby," she said.

My baby? When was the last time she called me that? My baby? Am I just a baby in a man's body? Start the car. Start the car!

"Good-bye, Mama," he said. "I'll call you when I get there."

He rolled the car out to the end of the driveway, waving to her as he did.

He had a map of Georgia and one of Tennessee sitting on the passenger seat.

He turned on the radio. *"That's the night when the lights went out in Georgia...that's the night they hung an innocent man...Don't trust your life to no backwoods southern lawyer..."*

He pulled out of Athens, on the loop, and headed west on Route 29.

He was singing at the top of his lungs when he saw the blinking red lights come up behind him and heard the siren.

He pulled over.

CHAPTER 36

What's Next?

Bobby was confused.

What now? What will I do, now that I can't play baseball anymore? It's all I know. No one's going to hire a cripple. No one's going to want me. Where do I belong? How will I live?

I can't let them see me cry. I need to get out of here. I can't stay in a nursing home! I am only 20 years old.

He thought about the times he'd rounded the bases in high school, the times he had struck out batters and thrown runners out at first base. Damn, I was good. And fast.

But he had been arrogant, too. In the months since the accident, he had come to realize that as well. He had little in the way of support from any kind of a family. His mother tried hard to get him what he needed, equipment-wise. She worked two, sometimes three, jobs, to provide for him and Charlie.

But his dad had done nothing. And now that he might have an insurance settlement in his future, he was sure the bum would show up for a piece of that pie, the same way he tried to get some of Bobby's signing bonus.

Who *was* going to pay for this place, anyway? Someone told Bobby that it cost $90 a day to stay here. That added up fast. Would whatever he got from the bus company's insurance pay for it?

He felt a steady stream of tears rolling down his cheeks, leaving crooked, shiny paths on his skin. He tasted the salt in his own tears, making it feel almost like it could be blood, running onto his chin and then to his neck.

It might as well be blood, he thought.

Because I'm wounded, inside and out.

Someone might as well stab me until I die.

What do I have to live for? I lived for baseball. Baseball was me and I was it.

Baseball is dead to me now, as dead as my legs, as dead as the bus on the side of the road.

CHAPTER 37

Help Wanted?

I wake up one morning—I think it's still morning—after sleeping for what seems like a long time. I know I can't go on living like this.

The Filly gives me money and I spend it. Dad is pissed off at me because I'm just hanging around the house, watching TV and then going out with Terry and Eddie at night.

Dad hates Terry and Eddie. "Bums! They're bums!" he says.

"They have jobs, Dad," I always defend them. Sure, they're just part-time jobs, but at least they're working.

"They're still bums! You need different friends. Why did you hook up with them, anyway? They're just bums. Whatever money they earn, they drink or smoke away. Is that what you want your life to be? Is it?"

No.

"Why don't you sign up for some college classes at Quincy Junior College, dear?" The Filly asks. "You could take some basic classes. It might be a nice place for you to explore college."

"Ma, you know I'm not college material," I reply. "Just ask Debbie. She'll tell you I'm just a dumb jock. Besides, what the hell would I study in college?"

"I'm just trying to give you some ideas, Jimmy, so you can improve your life."

I tone down my voice. I shouldn't be fresh to her. "Yeah, Ma, I know. I just don't think I'm cut out for college."

"Then what are you cut out for?" she asks. "You're not cut out for sitting around and watching TV all day long, I'm sure of that."

Wow. That's as close to an insult as you'll get from The Filly. She knows I'm bored. She knows I should be out jogging and working out.

"Yeah, Ma, you're probably right. I just need to think about this some more," I say. "I'm gonna go look for a job today. I know I've been talking about it for a long time, but today's the day."

"Where? You don't have a car. Where will you go?" she asks.

"I'm going to Mister Donut, down on Bridge Street, then I'm going up to the Volkswagen place. Maybe they have something I can do up there. It's not too far," I reply.

"Oh, those are good ideas, Jimmy. It shows me that you are thinking. It would be nice if you were able to make your own spending money, too."

This is the first time she's mentioned that I should earn my own money. I do have that signing bonus in the bank that I haven't touched. I don't want to get into that money unless it's a real emergency. I want to save it.

She smiles and goes into the kitchen, humming an unrecognizable tune.

I still can't fathom she told my dad to choose between her or baseball.

Dad's hands no longer look as if they belong to a baseball player; they're rough, calloused, swollen. His wedding ring no longer fits on his finger because his hands are working hands now, not those of someone who cherishes his hands as the tools of his trade on the baseball mound.

Dad's hands seem to have difficulty turning the pages when he reads *The Patriot-Ledger* every day. They are engorged, with crooked joints and stubs of fingernails. But he remains devoted to his job so he can put food on the table and pay the mortgage, and so The Filly doesn't have to get a job.

Debbie had a scholarship to pay for her college when she got a bachelor's degree, and now she has another one to pay for her graduate work. She's going Ivy League this time. I keep reminding myself that I have a sister who's going to Harvard.

Debbie is wicked smart.

Donna was good in school, too, but not at the top of the class like Debbie was. I know she'll be a great nurse. She cares a lot about people and their feelings.

So what *can* I do? I could make donuts at Mister Donut, I guess. I just want to make some money so The Filly and Dad don't have to give me anything, and get myself back to playing baseball next season.

I need to get myself up off the couch and moving, too. I think I should call my old coach from high school. Maybe he has some ideas.

Or maybe I could call Cesar. Yeah.

That's what I'll do.

CHAPTER 38

Do You Know How Fast
You Were Going?

Bud watched in the sideview mirror as a tall, slim police officer, wearing silver aviator-style sunglasses and high riding boots up to his knees headed his way.

The lights on top of the patrol car were flashing continuously, although the siren had been turned off.

It felt to Bud as if it took him a good five minutes to get to the driver's side window.

He slightly tilted the sunglasses down over his nose to reveal a small part of his piercing blue eyes.

"Son...Do you know how fast you were going?"

"I...I...I think I was going 50, sir," Bud responded.

"License and registration."

Bud leaned to the left of his seat to get his wallet from his right hip pocket.

Bud tilted toward the glove compartment, where he kept his registration, and pushed the button. It was stuck.

"Sir, I have to bang on the glove box. It's stuck."

"Thanks for the warning, son."

Bud hit the glove compartment, hard, on the lock, and it popped open.

He rifled through papers to find the registration. *There it is! Thank you, God!*

He reached over to the window and handed it to the officer. "There you go, sir."

The officer mumbled and went back to his own car. The lights were still flashing.

The officer came back, slowly again, clicking his boots on the pavement, again, but this time, on his way back to the driver's side window, he stopped and kicked in the left rear taillight. Bud heard the glass break, and he couldn't figure out what had happened.

"You got a taillight out, son" the officer said. "You gotta get that fixed. It's illegal. You can't drive much farther with a busted taillight."

"But, sir, it wasn't..."

"You got a busted taillight, hear me, son? You take this heap up to Stitham, 'bout half a mile up the road, and go to Jeeter's Garage. My friend, Jeeter, he'll fix it for you right quick. And you owe me fifty dollars for speeding."

"How fast was I going, sir?"

"Doesn't matter. You owe me fifty bucks."

Bud remembered that the hundred dollars his mother gave him. He sighed and reached into his wallet, counted out fifty dollars and handed it to the officer.

"May I have a receipt for this, sir?"

The officer let out a full-blown belly laugh. "You want a receipt? You think I carry receipts in my police car? You a joker or something?"

"No, sir, I just..."

"You just what? You don't trust me that I'm giving you a fair fine for breaking the law in my town? You want me to put you in jail and you can take it up with the judge? You gettin' off easy, son."

"No, sir, I do not want to go to jail."

"So get goin', down to Jeeter's, and get that taillight fixed. You hear?"

"Yes, sir."

Bud started the car and drove about half a mile, and, sure enough, there was Jeeter's Garage, on the right, and Jeeter was waiting for him.

"How y'all doing?" Jeeter asked. "Can I he'p you?"

"I have a broken taillight," Bud said. "Can you fix it for me?"

"Yup. We get a lot of those around here."

I bet you do. I bet you do. And I bet you have taillight parts for many different types of cars, just waiting in the back of this crummy garage.

"How much will it cost to have this done?" Bud asked. "I'm on my way to college, and I'm on kind of a tight budget."

"I'd say fifty dollars will do it," Jeeter said, and flashed Bud a smile, showing off a mouth that was missing six or seven teeth in important places. "Yep. That's what it'll cost ya."

It's going to be a long trip to Nashville.

It took Jeeter less than ten minutes to replace the red glass panel on the car's left taillight. "See? Good as new!" he announced to Bud.

"Yes, I see," Bud replied. "Can I get a receipt?"

"Receipt? Son, I don't give no receipts! No guarantees, no receipts! You just gotta have faith that I did the work right. Yep. Jeeter does the work right! If you stop by this way again, I can fix anything you got!"

CHAPTER 39

Preparing to Leave Clarence

The Brothers of Mercy case manager, Marie, was about forty, five feet tall and weighed about 100 pounds. She had short-cropped brown, curly hair with a few flecks of gray. She was kind, compassionate—and firm.

Bobby wheeled into her office. He didn't really like the wheelchair, but he was getting more adept at maneuvering around corners and backing up. His strong arms could almost lift him in and out of bed.

"Come in a little closer," Marie said. "I'll move the chairs. We'll save that one chair for Bernadette."

"She's coming?" he asked. "Is that a good sign or a bad sign?"

"I'll let you decide," Marie said. "But before she gets here, I want to commend you on the progress you have made since you came here."

"But are you kicking me out?" He chuckled a bit.

Bernadette walked in. "Hello, Bobby! Hello, Marie! It's a beautiful day, isn't it?"

Bobby looked out the window, and it was a dreary day, but every day to Bernadette was a beautiful day. Outside, it was what he would describe as very western New York—overcast, dingy, looking as if it would rain at any minute, or maybe even drop some snow or sleet. But none of this bothered Bernadette.

"Have a seat, Bernadette. We saved one for you," Marie said.

"As both of you know, our goal from the beginning was to get Bobby to the point where he could become independent enough to be transferred to a place where he could live on his own. I've been talking to a friend of mine in New York City, and, although we tried to find a place for you in Yonkers, near your mother and brother, we couldn't find anything for you there.

We found something in Flushing, near Shea Stadium. It's an independent apartment with built-in rails and lowered sinks, and, maybe most importantly, an elevator to get you to your apartment. It only has four floors, but you won't need the elevator. The place we have for you is on the first floor.

"The issue now, though, is getting you from Clarence to Flushing. I don't think you want to take the bus…"

Bobby cut her off. "No way! I'm not getting on one of those again!"

"We could get you on the train. It's a little bit more difficult to fly. We also have a volunteer who works here who used to live in New York City. He said he would drive you, as long as you can use some of your own money to pay for the gas. Would that be feasible?"

Bobby replied, "Let me think about it."

"Okay," Marie said. "The one advantage of that would be that Bernadette could ride along with you and could return when he came back to Buffalo. He lives in Buffalo."

"Can you ask me tomorrow, Marie? I need to think about it overnight."

He was surprised by how much he enjoyed talking to these two.

He soaked in the attention Bernadette gave him.

Before that chance encounter at the bus station, the only time anyone had taken notice of him and his talents had been when he was a baseball player, and those days were gone.

CHAPTER 40

An Apartment in Flushing

The case manager from New York, Michelle, was on the phone with Bobby. She had the apartment lined up for him, near Shea Stadium. It was completely handicapped-accessible, and, as Marie said, on the first floor.

"It sounds good, Michelle," he said.

"I have an 'in' with the manager. I told her about you. She has several younger people there, too. Many of the places like this are for the elderly, but this one has some people who are about the same age as you."

"Yippee," Bobby said. "A bunch of cripples my same age. That should be fun."

"Oh, stop!" she said. "Stop having a pity party. We're trying to help you. Don't you want to be helped?"

"Yup. Yup. Yup. Help is what I want," he answered, but rolled his eyes.

Yeah, I want help. I want my legs to work. Know anyone who has some fairy dust they can sprinkle on my spinal cord to fix it? I mean, that's the kind of help I want and need. I don't want to move into a handicapped-accessible apartment with guys "my own age." I want to be able to pitch and run the bases. Oh, how about you, Michelle?

"Don't be sarcastic with me, Bobby. I know you're frustrated, believe me, I do. But this is a good placement," she said.

"Yup, a good placement," he repeated.

She let out a heavy, audible sigh. "Don't mock me, Bobby."

"What? I'm not mocking you. I'm trying to figure this whole thing out. Where do I belong? What am I going to do with my life? Where do I live? What do I do? I know I can't stay here at Brothers of Mercy. That's all.

They're trying to kick me out. They say that I don't need any more rehabilitation. I think they hate me."

"They don't hate you, Bobby, but there are regulations—"

"Yeah, sure, regulations. I've heard that before, too. Regulations for bus companies that can't pay out their insurance claims. Regulations for lawyers who keep this stuff locked up in court..."

Another long sigh at the end of the phone. "Bobby...I am trying to get things set up for you. I have it all worked out. But if you don't want to go live there, I'm sure I can find someone else to take the apartment. These places aren't easy to find."

Stop being a jerk! She's making an effort for you. You gotta believe that. What are you afraid of? Going back to the city?

"i-I-I-I," he stuttered. "I know they're scarce, and I know I should be grateful, but..."

"Are you afraid to live on your own?" she asked.

"Maybe..."

"What are you afraid of? Maybe we can address your concerns."

"I-I-I-don't know, exactly, but how do I get food? How do I get around? I can't get into the subway or on the ell train on my own," he said, slowly.

"That's why you need a case worker," she replied, "and that's what I'm trying to tell you. Here in New York, we have transportation services that you have to sign up for when you have medical appointments or need to go shopping. You just make a phone call. That's all."

Why should I believe you? You're just a voice on the end of a phone line. I don't know you. You don't know me. You don't know how much I lost. You have no idea what I'm dealing with.

"Yup, yup, yup," he said. "I'll be in the city with my trusty wheels in two days. How should I get to your office?"

"Take a taxi. Get a receipt. I'll reimburse you for the cost," she said.

A taxi. How do taxis respond to cripples? Do they even know how to fold down one of these contraptions?

"Awright, I got it," he said. "I'll see you then."

"Good. I'm anxious to meet you," she said.

"Okay."

He was anxious to meet her, too.

He needed to see the woman sending him off to live in a box.

CHAPTER 41

Mister Donut

I drag myself out of bed and walk slowly to the bathroom. I'm going to start the job hunt at the donut shop and then work my way up the street to the Volkswagen dealership. If I can't get hired at either of those places, I'll head up Bridge Street, toward the Fore River Bridge, staying on the bus line.

If I get something at Mister Donut, I can walk to work. Good for training. I have to start somewhere. Just about the only exercise I've gotten since I got home is sneaking out to the little patch of woods behind Old Man Little's house to drink beer.

Terry, Eddie and I have walked to Wessagusset Beach a few times to hang out on the seawall. None of us is old enough, on paper, to drink. But we can handle our liquor, even when Terry brings vodka on top of the beer.

I do feel a little hung over today. As I walk into the bathroom, which smells girly to me, with its lingering perfume and shampoo smells my sisters and The Filly leave behind, I feel a little sick in my stomach.

I start the water running in the shower and notice that the flowery shower curtain seems to match the perfume in the air. That's about right. The Filly loves her flowers. Sigh. I adjust the water, throw off my pajamas, and hop in. Dial soap. Head and Shoulders shampoo. That's all you need. You can smell clean with those two ingredients. You don't need cologne or after-shave lotion.

I finish the shower, grab a towel, and start to shave. I look in the mirror. *Man, look at those bags under your eyes, Jimmy! You look like you're 30 years old! Maybe even 40! Wow! What have you been doing to yourself? Splash some cold water on your eyes! You need help!*

I blink my eyes a few times, step back, throw some cold water on my face, and shake my head, like a dog that just came out of a lake.

I slap my face, then reach for the shaving cream. I shake the can, squirt it on my hands and spread it on my face. It reminds me of whipped cream that comes in a can, and of the days when Debbie, Donna and I used to have fights with the canned whipped cream in the backyard. We would laugh and laugh, and spray each other with the white stuff, and then The Filly would come home and find us rolling around in the grass, laughing hysterically. She would chide us in her gentle Filly way, and remind us that she had bought that whipped cream to use on some Jell-O dish she had planned to make for the priest at St. Jerome's Church. She would shake her head and say something like, "But it's okay, if it allows my babies to have fun, I can just go to the store and buy some more!"

I go back to my little room and pull out a pair of khakis and a short-sleeved shirt. I refuse to consider wearing a tie. I return to the bathroom and look in the mirror again. At least now I look semi-alive. I open the medicine cabinet and pull out a comb. I really should have gotten a haircut.

"Ma! I'm leaving!" I yell out to The Filly, who's in the kitchen.

"I hope you find a good job."

A good job? Putting donuts in a box and pouring coffee? I think being a professional baseball player is a good job. Or maybe being an engineer who builds bridges like the Fore River or Mystic River Bridge. Or maybe being a doctor. But working at the donut shop?

"Okay, Ma, I'll let you know."

I walk down Green Street and turn the corner onto Bridge Street, and, there it is: Mister Donut. The parking lot is full, as it always is. This place is trying to compete with Dunkin' Donuts, which is starting to expand from its original place on the Southern Artery in Quincy. I don't care which brand it is; this one is within walking distance of my house.

I notice that they have a sign at the counter that they are accepting applications. I get at the back of the line and wait my turn.

"May I help you?" asks a cute young woman, maybe 20 or so, behind the counter.

"Yeah," I respond. "I'd like to pick up a job application."

"So you'd like to work here? That would be nice."

Is she flirting with me? She is wicked cute, and she could be a distraction, if I were to get a job here.

"Well, I'd like to *apply*," I say, "and then we'll see what happens."

She bats her eyelashes at me a bit. "I'll get the manager out here. He'll want to talk to you. Hey, Candy? Can you take the register for a minute? I need to go get Al."

"Sure!" a voice from the end of the counter calls out.

I stand to the side so that Candy can wait on the customers who were behind me in the line. There was quite a line in this busy place. Do people *really* like donuts *this* much?

The first woman returns. "Al, this is...I didn't get your name..."

"Jimmy...Jimmy Bailey."

"Jimmy Bailey? The baseball player?" Al asks.

"Yes. I'm home from my first season of minor-league baseball, and I need an off-season job," I say.

"I followed you when you were in high school, and then when you got drafted," Al says. "You went with The Expos, right? Over to their Single-A in Jamestown, New York..." Then he paused for a few seconds. "Okay. Let's get back to the real world. What kind of job are you looking for?"

"Anything that's available," I respond. I didn't think anyone would remember my past baseball track record, even here in my home town.

"Well, we always have counter positions available, like the one that Patty here has, but we have baking positions, too, where you'd be in the back making donuts. We have a few other options, like unloading trucks that come in with supplies a couple of times a week," Al explains. "Any of those interest you?"

"I guess I could do any of those jobs," I respond, "but I think that the unloading job sounds like the one that would fit me best."

"Okay," Al says. "Fill out the application, bring it back later today, and I'll talk to the owner. I can get back to you tomorrow. Does that work for you?"

"Sure. Sure," I say. "That would be fine. Nice meeting you, Al, Patty." I nod and start walking. The Filly had told me to smile, so I do. Maybe a half-smile.

Unloading things from the truck into the donut shop. I can do that. But wait! What if I hurt my arm when I'm unloading stuff? Maybe I should ask to get a cashier's job. But wait! What would I do if some of the guys I used to pitch to, used to mow down when they were at the plate and I was on the mound, come in to buy donuts, and I'm wearing one of those silly paper hats, and they recognize me? How embarrassing would that be? So maybe I should ask to learn how to make the donuts? But wait! What if I burn my hand taking donuts out of the oven? If I could learn to only use my left hand to take the donut trays out of the oven, maybe it would be safer. I'm not sure I can remember that, though.

So much to think about. Maybe working at the donut shop isn't the best idea. But what is? I need to make some money during the off season. Not only do I need to get some moola together to keep me in beer, but if I want to go out to the movies or anything like that, I have to earn something to pay for that. My parents can't keep paying for my little hobbies. I could never afford to take a girl out to dinner. And Dad has said that if I can't help with the car insurance, I can't use his car.

Donut shop it is.

I head home and to fill out the application. It shouldn't take too long. I've never really held a job, so there's not much job history to account for on the application. I guess I need to put down what I've done in baseball. That's my real profession.

CHAPTER 42

Bobby Returns to the Big Apple

"Bobby, is everything packed and ready to go? Does everyone at the other end know you're flying in today?" Bernadette asked him.

"My Ma knows," he replied, "and I suppose she's told Charlie, but I'm not going home to her apartment."

"So let's go. You should try to find your guys and say good-bye before you take off," she said.

"Yeah, Mark and Jonesy, for sure. We had some fun here, but it will be good to be on the outside again," he said. "And I have to find Hank, too. He's a good guy."

"Speak of the devil!" Bernadette said.

"Hey, you!" Hank yelled. "Goin' somewhere?"

Bobby looked up and smiled a full-toothed grin. "Hey, man! You gonna miss me when I'm gone?"

Hank mimed crying and wiping away tears. "I'll never get over you! We had a good thing going!"

How did this happen to me? How did I make friends? I never had friends in high school or even on my baseball teams. Now I can't even walk and I have friends. What is this?

"Yeah, you'll forget me as soon as I wheel out the door," he said, specifically looking at Hank.

Hank reached out his hand and grabbed Bobby's. "No, kid, I won't forget you. You're a piece of work, you are, and I've had fun having you here. Frustration some days, but you're a good guy. Mostly!"

He laughed again and gave Bobby's hand a good strong shake, then bent down to hug him in his chair. "I'll miss you, man. Truly, I will."

What, am I crying? What, am I upset that I'm leaving a blooming nursing home?

"Yeah, I'll miss you, too, man. You made it easier to be here. I thought it was going to be all old ladies sitting with afghans on their laps, but you and Mark and Jonesy—real guys—real friends. Thanks for everything."

"It makes my job easier, you know, to have residents like you to laugh with—and laugh *at*!" Hank said. "C'mon, let's go. Bernadette, you ready?"

"Sure. You got all his stuff? He sure accumulated a bunch of stuff while he was here."

"Happens all the time," Hank said. "Who's going to be the chauffeur, you or me, Bernadette?"

"You do the honors, Hank," she replied.

"Ok, let's do it," Hank said, "and we'll pop a few wheelies on the way out."

Down the hall they rolled, waving to nurses and aides as they passed. Bernadette had trouble keeping up with them, as they zipped from side to side to avoid other residents as they laughed and hooted like little boys running around in the backyard on the first day of spring.

Finally, they reached the front door. "Well, this is it, kiddo."

This time, Bobby took Hank's hand into both of his.

"I owe you big, man, I owe you big." He felt tears again.

"You owe me nothing," Hank replied, "except to get out in that world and show them what you can do."

Bobby wheeled himself out through the opening of the automatic door, where a van was waiting for him and his wheelchair. The driver helped him make the transfer from the wheelchair into a seat in the van. He strapped Bobby into the seat and then called to Bernadette.

"Ma'am, you can get into the front passenger seat and come along with us," the driver said.

"Bernadette, are you coming to the airport with us?" Bobby asked.

"You betcha!" she replied. "I just wish I could go all the way to New York City with you. I haven't been there in years. Maybe after you get settled, I can figure out a way to visit you out there."

"Hey, that's a great idea. We'll work on that. Bring Hank, Mark and Jonesy with you, too," he said.

"Wouldn't that be a party?"

"Yup. Yup. Yup. And in the tiny apartment they're giving me, it would be like hanging out in a phone booth!"

It was an art, really, being able to place someone into a wheelchair skill-fully and without dropping him, Bobby thought, almost like throwing a pitch where you want it to go. Bobby was amazed at how easily it seemed to take place, when they reached the airport.

Bernadette, too, noticed it was effortless, the way the driver knew exactly what to do.

"Wow, smooth, bro," Bobby said. "Thanks for helping me out."

The driver gathered Bobby's suitcase and duffel bag and helped him check in at the curb.

He walked back over to the car as Bobby and Bernadette remained, almost frozen, as they looked at the Brothers of Mercy logo on the side of the van.

They were good to me. I didn't expect it, but they were good to me. Mercy. Really. They showed me mercy. Before I met Bernadette I never knew mercy. Or love. Love and mercy.

Bernadette grabbed the handles of the wheelchair and said, "I'll take over from here. Thanks for all your help." She pulled the chair toward her and then away, focusing on getting to the main terminal.

Buffalo International was small, compared with airports of other major cities. Bernadette liked that. She didn't have to worry about getting con-fused in finding the right gate or a ladies' room. She could read the clear signs and could ask people for help. Everyone here in Buffalo was helpful. Everyone.

She pushed Bobby up to the counter, where he leaned up to speak to the clerk, who stamped a couple of things onto Bobby's ticket and handed it back to him. "Gate A-7," then asked, "Do you need any other assistance?"

"I haven't traveled on a plane since—since I've been using a wheelchair, so I don't really know what I need," he replied.

She thought for a minute, and he detected an almost patronizing look from her as she peered down at him over the counter. Bernadette was ner-vously clicking her fingers together.

"I will call down to the gate and ask them to pre-board you on the flight, and to help you with your chair," she said. "The gate agent will assist you with whatever you need. I have never worked a gate, so I'm not really sure."

"I'm pretty sure that he'll get what he needs when he gets there," Bernadette piped up.

Once again, she pulled the chair toward her before pushing it ahead. "Bobby, are you okay?"

He let out a long, audible sigh.

"I guess it's hitting me that I'm going to be in this chair for the rest of my life, and people are going to be looking down at me forever, and that I have to figure out a way to get used to this."

She stopped rolling the chair. She bent down and talked to him face to face. "Bobby, no one says you have to get used to it. What you have to start doing is loving yourself. When you were playing baseball, you loved yourself as a baseball player. Now you have to learn to love yourself as Bobby. You're a really cool guy, but you have to believe that. The rest of us know it. Now you need to start working on it."

The rest of you know it? Who are the rest of you? I'm a really cool guy? Love myself? What is this crap?

Bobby was speechless. He couldn't respond to Bernadette's remarks.

"Just keep driving," he finally said.

She resumed pushing the wheelchair, this time in silence.

Bobby leaned over onto his clenched fist, looking like a baseball-capped Rodin's *The Thinker* in a wheelchair, being pushed by a 70-something woman dressed in layers of clothing and wearing flat shoes. He didn't know whether to laugh or cry.

"Well, here we are," she announced. "Here's your gate."

"Yup. Yup. Yup. Have to talk to the gate agent."

Bobby plunked the ticket folder on the counter.

"I see you're flying to New York City, LaGuardia. Big airport. Have you ever been there before, sir?"

"Yup. Yup. Yup. I grew up in the city," Bobby replied. "But I haven't been there since I've been riding in this beast."

The gate agent didn't seem to know how to respond. "Oh—oh—okay," he said. "Well, we will see that you will be pre-boarded before anyone else, and we will have your chair folded and placed in the baggage compartment. Then we will retrieve it at the other end and have it ready for you at LaGuardia. As soon as the flight crew arrives, I will introduce you to the stewardess who will take care of everything."

"That will be great," Bernadette said. "Isn't that terrific, Bobby?"

Yeah. Terrific. Fly on a plane. Sit in a seat. Don't forget to fasten your seatbelt. Hope the person sitting next to you doesn't see your catheter bag. Hope the bag doesn't bust in flight. At least no one has to help you to the bathroom. One good thing, huh?

"I have no idea what I'm getting into. All I know is, the woman from the Jewish Family Services says she's got an apartment ready for me in Flushing, and I'm going from the airport to my new home, sight unseen. I've got to figure out how to take care of myself, and my legs don't work. I pee in a bag. I have no job. My mother and brother live in Yonkers in a seventh-floor walk-up. I can't visit them there. Who knows if they'll come to me?"

"Bobby, I don't know what to say. I just wish you wouldn't leave me feeling like I had failed you. I am looking at you and thinking that you need something I don't have to give."

"Bernadette, you have given me more than you will know. I don't have the right words to tell you right now. Maybe some day I will."

"Mr. Mangino," the gate agent called out, "Please come to the desk."

Bobby wheeled himself over to the desk, where the gate agent said, "Mr. Mangino, this is Barbara McTeele, and she will assist you in getting to your destination."

"Glad to meet you, Mr. Mangino. Happy to help."

"Bobby. You can call me Bobby."

"Thank you. And you can call me Barbara or Barb. But some of my friends call me Bobby, too."

"Take good care of my Bobby," Bernadette instructed Barbara. "He has been through a lot, and he's getting ready to begin a whole new chapter in his life."

"I will make sure he gets everything he needs, ma'am," Barbara said. "And it's time for him to pre-board the airplane."

Bernadette bent down to hug Bobby one last time. She put her arms tightly around him, bear-hug style, and didn't want to let go.

"Bobby, you've been the grandson I never had. I will come to New York to see you. I promise."

"And you have been the grandma I never had, Bernadette. I'll never forget what you did for me. Keep in touch. I'll call you when I get a phone."

Wheeling him down the ramp to the airplane, Barbara asked, "Is she a relative?" Barbara asked.

"Sorta," Bobby said. "We adopted each other. We've been through a lot together."

CHAPTER 43

First Day on the Job

Today is my first day at the donut job. Al told me to show up at 8 AM, and I'm early.

I take the right turn onto Bridge Street and walk past the cars in the parking lot, through the front door and crisscross my way around the long line waiting for coffee and donuts.

This place is nuts. How many donuts can people buy? How much coffee can people drink?

Candy sees me. She nods to me and mouths the words, "Open the latch and go in the back."

"Hey, Jimmy, over here!" Al says. "Glad to see you made it. We've got a lot of work to do. We have a bunch of boxes to open, and there will be a truck coming in soon. We have to unload that one, too."

"What should I do, Al? Where should I start?" I ask.

"Over here, over here," he points to a big stack of cardboard. "See, they have numbers on them. We have to open them in order, according to the numbers. They have stuff in them we need, like napkins, plastic knives and forks, donut boxes, bags, stuff like that. We take them out in order so we know what we've already done. Capeesh?"

"Yes, I've got it," I tell him. *Capeesh reminds me of Russ.*

Al and I work to open the boxes, in order, and we make amazing progress. As we empty them, we throw the boxes out the back door. The sea of cardboard has gone out with the tide and in its place is an orderly stack of napkins, plastic tableware, flat donut boxes that will be assembled at the front counter, and white, waxed-paper bags with the Mister Donut logo on the front. The next shipment will contain paper coffee cups and stirrers, Al says.

Then I hear the "beep, beep, beep" of a truck, an 18-wheeler, backing up to the door.

"Must be the cups," Al says. "We finished just in the knick of time."

We go outside, into the light, and the sun feels good on my face. I take in a deep breath and can smell Wessagusset Beach, about half a mile away. I look up and see a stray seagull on his way to the beach.

We only have to take out about a-third of the boxes in the truck. The rest are going to other Mister Donut shops in the area. I'm just as glad, because getting up and down on the truck is tiring out my legs. I guess I'm not in as good shape as I thought I was. This is a pretty good workout. I'm feeling muscles and tendons I forgot I had.

"Hey, Joey, thanks," Al says, as the little trucker gets back in the cab.

We go back inside. I feel as if I've worked for a week.

It's 10:48 AM.

Al gives me my official Mister Donut shirt and paper hat. Must be legit.

I count and stack, count and stack. Everything looks great, and then a new truckload of supplies arrives, and we start all over again. It's like that all day.

Al also trained me to work at the front and help the girls out when it gets busy at the cash register. Candy and the rest of the crew are so efficient that it makes me feel clumsy, like I'm in the way. They seem to know what their customers want, even before they open their mouths to place the order. Mostly, they ask me to assemble boxes for a dozen donuts.

When it gets slow, I go back to unloading cartons and organizing supplies.

And watching the clock.

I received my first paycheck after a week.

It was a whopping $68.29, after taxes. I only worked 28 hours. Al says he will give me some more hours, now that I have an idea of what I am doing.

Up front with the cashiers, I have to wear that ridiculous paper hat, with the Mister Donut logo on either side.

The first time I actually worked the cash register, I saw a bunch of guys from Braintree who had stopped on their way to Nantasket to get coffee and donuts.

"Hey, isn't that Jimmy the pitcher who used to be such a big baseball star?"

I keep looking at the floor.

"Hey! Aren't you Jimmy Bailey? Didn't you used to pitch for Weymouth High? And Weymouth Babe Ruth? I thought you signed a contract with a major league team—was it The Expos?"

I look up and see that he was the left fielder for Braintree High. He couldn't hit anything I had.

"You're not such a big man now, are you, Bailey?"

They all laugh.

Candy asks them to leave. "You're annoying our customers," she says.

"So the guy in the paper hat isn't annoying them? He's annoying *me!*" says one of the guys.

After they leave, Candy said, "Let's go in the back room."

We walk past the other two girls and behind a few boxes I still need to empty.

"What was that all about?" she asks.

"Those guys—I used to play ball against them," I reply.

"Are you embarrassed that they came in here, trying to make you screw up?" she asks.

"You think they were trying to make me screw up? I thought they were trying to make me look stupid, because I always made them look stupid when they were batting against me."

"Jimmy, you can't let customers get to you. You either work here and act proud that you're part of the team, or you decide that you need to find somewhere else to work. I'm not going to talk to Al about this, but me and the girls, we need your help, not to have to rescue you from a bunch of jerks," she says.

"I got it."

"Okay," she says. "And Jimmy..."

"Yeah?"

"Watch out for cranky Father McElroy. He can be a lot worse than a bunch of ballplayers from Braintree."

"Got it."

CHAPTER 44

Vanderbilt University

Bud heaved a big, slow sigh of relief as he entered the winding drive-way into the campus of Vanderbilt.

The place was as impressive as it looked in the college bro-chures—expansive emerald-green lawns between stately buildings with large white Doric columns, just like those at Lindenwood. Perfectly pruned rose bushes of different colors, interspersed with begonias, impatiens and daisies.

Bud's grandmother would have loved it. She'd have gone out of her way to find and compliment the gardeners and groundskeepers.

He felt her presence was with him today, on this campus, just as she was whenever he was at Lindenwood.

He parked his car in the lot to which he was directed, locked it, and headed to the freshman orientation area. The place was daunting. Did he have the academic credentials, the wherewithal, to do this?

The admissions people determined I am qualified to be here.

A young woman wearing a Vanderbilt name tag that read "Mary Ann" walked up to him and asked, "May I help you?" She said she worked in the admissions office.

"Hi, Mary Ann," he said. "Yes, can you tell me where I should start? I just got here."

"Okay, so you just have to find the table that's marked with your last name, and you should stand in that line. They'll tell you what to do next," Mary Ann said.

"Thanks, Mary Ann, I appreciate your help," he replied.

He stood in line. The guy in front of him turned around and asked where he was from.

"Athens, Georgia," he replied. "How about you?"

"Maryville, Tennessee, right outside of Knoxville" he said. "My name's John Peterson. And you?"

"Bud Prescott," he replied.

"Next!" the woman at the table called out.

John moved up to the table.

He was in a gymnasium of some sort. People from various administrative offices were darting back and forth, like bees returning to their hives, ready to drop off their honey after a busy day.

"Next!" the woman at the table yelled again.

"Cameron Prescott."

"Prescott...Prescott...Ah, yes. Here you are. You are in East House. Here are the keys to your room. You have to go have an ID photo taken."

She scrambled around for a few seconds and came up with a manila envelope with his name in the upper left-hand corner.

"This envelope contains everything you need—your schedule, your parking permit for your car, your health clinic information, and your food card. Any questions?"

"No, ma'am, I don't have any questions...Oh, wait, maybe one. Where is the parking lot for my car?"

"It's behind the student union building. Look at your map in your packet and you will find it," she replied.

I wonder if my roommate Tom Cooney has arrived. I am anxious to meet him. I hope we get along. I wonder if he's a baseball player, too. Or another type of athlete.

He walked out of the orientation building and figured out the pathway to East Hall, drove the car to the front door and pulled up to the entrance. A couple of guys came out and asked who he was.

"Bud Prescott," he replied, as he got out of the driver's seat and closed the door.

"Hey, I think you're my roommate. I'm Tom Cooney," said one.

"Hey, Tom!" Bud said. "I've been waiting to meet you."

"Same here," said Tom. "Let me help you unload this beast."

CHAPTER 45

Watch Out, Big Apple

Bobby looked out the window of the DC-9 heading to LaGuardia. The other seat was empty, as was half of the plane. He'd scored a first-class seat.

"This is your captain speaking. We should be on the ground in about twenty minutes."

Twenty minutes. I guess this is it. I don't even know if my mother will be there, waiting for me. I know I can get a cab to the Flushing address, if she doesn't show.

Barbara came by his seat and leaned down. "Bobby, it may take some time to get your own wheelchair when we land. I have asked that someone meet us at the gate with a wheelchair until we can get yours out."

"Whatever you think will work best," he said. He looked out the window again and watched as the ground began to come closer and closer.

As the plane dropped down to LaGuardia, he saw familiar sights. Shea Stadium. The Singer Bowl. The Unisphere from the 1964 World's Fair.

After they landed, he felt a big thunk as the plane's door opened and the hatch attached to the jetway. He looked up and two very large uniformed men were at his side, unbuckling his seat belt and carrying him out the door. It took less than a minute before he was in a wheelchair with the letters "LGA" on each side.

He sat on the side of the jetway, watching businessmen in suits, carrying briefcases and straightening their ties, walk faster and faster into the LaGuardia terminal. One tired-looking mother with two small children.

He looked down the jetway and saw people in their own little cocoons, not caring whether they bumped into others. They had places to go, people to see, trains and taxis to catch. It wasn't even rush hour, but they were hustling.

"Bobby? You ready?" Barbara asked, as she came up behind the wheelchair.

"We fly all over the country, and I see a lot of airports. This place and Chicago are the two craziest. Atlanta and Boston aren't too far behind, though," she added.

"I've never been anywhere else," he said. "Just here, then I took the bus to Jamestown to play ball. The Falcons took the bus to the places where we played. We didn't fly. The plane we flew in on was the first flight I ever took."

"Really? It was your maiden voyage?"

"Yup. Kinda funny, huh? My legs don't work, so I got wings."

CHAPTER 46

Surprise!

The grass on the Vanderbilt campus was groomed to an exquisite ball-park green, and gave off a sweet aroma. Bud relished it because it transported him mentally as if he were in a ballpark on game day. Sometimes he relied on the perfume of the grass to keep him centered.

Tom was an easy-going roommate; they got along well. But some of the other guys on their floor were downright rude—kids from wealthy families, who treated those they deemed beneath them with disdain and cruelty.

Despite his deep southern roots and connection to prominent Civil War leaders, Bud didn't tolerate people who looked down at other people who might not be as fortunate. *An accident of birth, that's all it is. How does the song go? There but for fortune, go you or I? It's a roll of the dice. Grandma always taught me that we're all people, everyone the same under the skin. No one is better or worse. Live your life that way. Give what you can, but only take what you need.*

Spoiled brats. That's what they are.

Tom Cooney wasn't a spoiled brat. His was a middle-class family in Arundel, Maryland. His father had been an Army engineer and his mother a teacher. He had two younger sisters and a Golden retriever. They had two cars and a house with a bath-and-a-half so that when his sisters were fussing over their make-up, they could be relegated to the half bath. Tom was the oldest; he'd been a football player in high school but destroyed his ACL while in a practice scrimmage. After surgery, he decided that was it, no more sports.

But he loved to watch football and baseball. He followed the University of Maryland Terrapins and the Atlanta Braves.

Tom was a raconteur, true to his Irish heritage, and got along with just about everyone. But he agreed with Bud about the kids who seemed to feel entitled.

"It's not as if they lack for anything in their lives, Bud. Why do they feel that they have to walk all over everyone else?"

Their educational interests were very different.

Tom was majoring in political science, with the plan of going to law school, while Bud was in the pre-med program, aiming to enroll in medical school if that baseball thing didn't work out.

Neither had a girfriend; both were too focused on school and career.

One October night, they sat in their dorm room, reading, when Bud answered a knock on the door.

"Hi, Bud. Did you miss me?"

Jenny Murphy stood in the hallway.

Tom looked up from his book.

Whoa, who is this? Bud never mentioned anyone to me.

Bud went out into the hall and closed the door behind him.

"Jenny, what are you doing here?" Bud asked.

"What? Don't you want to see me, Bud?"

"I just wasn't expecting you," he replied. "We can't have women in the room after midnight during the week."

"I wanted to surprise you. I haven't been able to stop thinking about you since you left Athens."

"So you made the drive up here? By yourself? Jenny, do you have any money? I mean, there are a couple of motels around here. I think we should try to find one where you could stay. You can't stay here in the dorm. Tom and I will get in trouble," he said.

"What do you have in mind, Bud?"

"I just want you to find a place to sleep and maybe we can get together for breakfast and lunch tomorrow, then we can talk about your trip back home."

She thought he'd be happy to see her, that he'd welcome her to stay the night with him. Instead, she'd found the only guy in the entire Volunteer State who worried about breaking his dorm rules.

"Okay, so where should I go?" she asked.

"I'll ask my roommate. He always knows what to do," Bud said.

He didn't know what this was all about. Sure, Jenny was a nice girl, but he wasn't about to get involved with anyone.

He opened the door and found Tom had fallen asleep on his bed.

"Wake up, roomie! I need you."

"Wha?" Tom asked.

"Here's the situation. My friend Jenny here is from my hometown. She came to visit me, but I didn't know she was coming. She needs a place to stay tonight. I told her she can't stay here because of the dorm rules. We need to find her a motel where she can stay for the night. Any ideas?"

"Give me a minute." Tom walked out the door.

"Where's he going?" Jenny asked.

"I don't know, but usually, when he asks me to give him a minute, he comes back with a solution," Bud said. "Why don't you sit down while we wait for him?"

She sat down at the swivel chair, right by the desk, and started to swing around. "Your room is nice," she said. "I decided not to start college this semester. I got a job at the animal hospital as a receptionist."

Tom came bursting back into the room and said, "I think I've got the answer. Jack down the end of the hall, he has a cousin who lives in town. She has an extra room. Jenny can stay with her tonight. It won't cost you anything, money-wise. Does that work?"

Bud could see in Jenny's face that she wasn't keen on staying with someone she didn't know.

"Yeah, we'll all go together," he said. "Tell you what, Jenny, I'll ride in your car and Tom can follow in mine, and I can ride back with him in my car."

He grabbed his keys and the three of them headed to the parking lot.

"Let's go."

CHAPTER 47

Wessagusset Beach

I tell The Filly I'm going out.

"Where the hell you going, Jimmy?" Dad asks. "You've got to work early in the morning. You need sleep."

"Now, now," The Filly says. "He's a grown boy. I'm sure he won't stay out too long, Jim."

"I need to get out of the house for a while, Dad, Ma. Just for a while."

"So you can go drinking? I know what you're doing, and you're pissing your life away. You think you worked so hard to get where you got, just to throw it all away, into a beer bottle?"

"I'm not throwing anything away, Dad," I say, "I just need a break."

"A break. A *break*? You need a break? A break from what? From working a high-stress job at the donut shop?"

"Now, James," The Filly intervenes, "We all need..."

"Mary, stay out of this!" Dad screams. "I will not watch him ruin his life with those deadbeats from high school. They'll never amount to anything. They'll never get out of this town."

He gets up and comes over to me. He puts his hands on my shoulders and squeezes.

"I'm not telling you this for my benefit. This is for your benefit and the benefit of your future. Do you even think you have a future?"

I remain silent.

"Are you working out? Are you running? Are you keeping up your physical activity? No, you're not. Your contract says you'll stay in shape."

He pokes me in the gut.

"What do you have to show? Nothing. Too many donuts!"

True.

"And too much beer! I know you've been getting it from Terry and Eddie. I just don't know who's supplying them."

Right again, Dad.

"So what do you have to say for yourself?"

"I don't know."

"That's right, you don't know. Because I'm dead right! You blow baseball, you blow your future. You got it?"

How does he know what Skip says to us? How does he know just the right buttons to push to make me feel like a failure?

I run past him, tempted to push him over, stomp up the stairs, go into my room, and slam the door. The slammed door holds up better than I am holding up. It has a crack in it now, but I feel broken.

I let him down.

He has placed so much of his trust, himself, in me, and I am giving him very little return on his investment.

Downstairs, I hear a low rumble of talk between Dad and The Filly. It sounds as if it could be an argument, although the tone is pretty civil.

The phone rings. "I'll get it!" I scream, and I run out to the hallway and pick up the phone. It's Terry.

"Bailey? We decided to go to the beach tonight. If you're coming, that's where we're going. Big bunch of us. We're leaving Eddie's house now."

"Uh, okay, Terry. Maybe, maybe not."

"Why? You chicken?"

"No, just had a little run-in with the folks here. May be better if I stay home."

"No better time to get out of the house, man," Terry says.

"Maybe. Maybe not. We'll see."

"Okay, you know where to find us. We'll be near the bath house."

After dinner, Dad goes to the living room to watch TV. The Filly asks me to forgive him.

"Oh, honey, he just loves you so much that he wants you to be the best you can be," she says. "He wants the same for your sisters, too, but he especially wants you to be a great baseball player."

"I know, Ma, I know. But I still have to be able to have some fun once in a while, too, and my friends here in Weymouth are maybe not what he wants me to be doing, but they're basically all I have here."

"Did you make friends in the baseball, too, dear?"

"I did, but they're pretty far away. One guy, you would like, Ma. Everyone liked him. His name is Bud Prescott. He's from Georgia and he's in college now. I should look him up some day, I guess. But now, I want to go out for a while. I'm going to walk down to the beach. I won't stay out late, Ma, honest, I won't."

I step outside to the sidewalk, and walk faster and faster, toward Wessagusset Beach.

I pass Pequot Road and I think I've gone by Pecksuot Road, too. I can smell the beach from here. I can just about taste the beer that I'm craving, too. Terry said they had supplies, and I am assuming that means beer. I can hear the waves breaking against the rocks over by the Weymouth Yacht Club to my left. The bath house is on the right, and the "h"-shaped dock where they teach swimming classes is straight ahead, in the water, bobbing up and down. It's mid-tide.

I see a bunch of people in the gully behind the bath house.

I walk over and find Terry and Eddie, and they are blasted drunk. They're laughing, hooting, pointing at me.

"What the hell took you so long? We're almost out of booze!" Eddie says.

Terry mumbles something. I don't think even he knows what he's saying.

Three other guys I've never seen before are also there. Everyone is smoking and drinking; some are smoking weed.

I reach for a beer and one of the guys I don't know grabs my hand—my pitching hand—and says, "So, it's the donut guy, and he thinks he can have a beer. Who invited you?"

"Terry and Eddie," I reply. "I hang with them all the time. Who the hell are you?"

"Never mind who I am. You didn't pay for this stuff, you get none of it."

"I have money here for Terry and Eddie, that's who I pay," I tell him. "Now let go of my hand."

I pull my hand away from him and go over to the inebriated Terry and Eddie.

"Hey, you guys, what's going on here? Why won't this guy let me have a beer?"

Terry mumbles, "Mmmm...Beer...gleee..."

Eddie says, "Some money here...Jimmy boy...come back..."

I should just leave. I only want one beer.

I turn to the guy who's guarding the beer. "I just want one beer. Here's my money."

I throw down a five-dollar bill.

"Don't treat me like I'm one of your underlings," he says. "I'm not a baseball fan. You can't impress me, just because you know how to throw a ball."

"Not trying to impress you," I say. "I'm trying to get a beer."

"Who says you're old enough to drink?" he asks me. "I say you're still a baby and can't hold your liquor, anyway."

I grab a beer and run down to the water. I pop the top off the can and start drinking.

The guy follows me and grabs me by the shoulders. He turns me around and decks me, knocking me down into the sand. The beer goes flying. My mouth is bleeding and I can't think. I stand back up and look at the guy. He hits me again.

I start hitting him and we go back and forth, back and forth. I get off a few good punches, and we're rolling around in the sand, trading punches, and I get off one good knee to his groin.

We roll closer to the water. The sand feels more wet. I'm now bleeding from my mouth and the side of my face. I can't think straight, but I'm still fighting. I try to break free from this guy, but he continues to hold on and hit me.

We roll into the water, and the waves slide gently into us. The salt water stings my face where I'm bleeding. I continue to hit him, trying to defend myself and get away from him. He still hangs on to me.

My clothes get heavier as we go deeper into the water. I finally break away from him. It feels like this has been going on for hours. I walk out onto the beach and collapse. I pass out in the sand.

I wake up as the tide is coming in and the water is making my body rise. I stand up and shake myself. I remember that I was fighting and that my face and mouth had been bleeding. I can feel that my face is swollen. I can't see anyone else around. I see the sky is beginning to brighten and day is about to begin.

I am in big trouble with my parents. I promised The Filly I wouldn't stay out late.

I stagger toward home. But I'm not drunk. I'm injured and every inch of my body hurts.

Just before I reach Bridge Street, a guy in a 1968 Pontiac GTO pulls over. It's a guy I went to high school with but barely knew. He was in the vocational school and learned to restore cars.

"Hey, Jimmy, you okay?" he asks. "Can I give you a ride home?"

"Sure, that would be great," I say. "I don't know what happened, but I think someone beat me up last night."

"Doesn't sound good. You look terrible. Do you want me to take you to the hospital?"

"No, just take me home. Do you remember where my parents live?"

"Down by St. Jerome's Church?"

"Yeah, head that way, and then I'll direct you," I say.

He drops me off at the house, and I drag myself up the steps.

Dad is sitting at the kitchen table. He has to be at work at 6 in the morning.

"Where the hell have you been? What have you done?"

"I-I-I was attacked by this guy and I defended myself, Dad."

"So who was it—Terry or Eddie?"

"It wasn't either one of them, but they were there. We were at the beach. Terry and Eddie were rip-roarin' drunk, and this guy I'd never seen before came after me. Punched me across the face, so I hit him back, and we went back and forth for a while, ended up in the water, and I passed out on the sand."

"Who was this guy?"

"I don't know. Never saw him before. Hope I never see him again."

"Go clean yourself up. You have to be at work in about two hours."

I stumble up the stairs to the bathroom. I look in the mirror. The guy who gave me a ride home was right. I look terrible. I feel even worse. How will I make it through eight hours at Mister Donut?

I start the shower. I try to convince myself that the warm water will feel good.

The water coming out of the showerhead smells so much better than the sea water at the beach, but it stings almost as bad as the salt water when it hits my skin. I look down and see bruises all over my chest, legs and even my feet.

Wow, that guy got me good. All I did was try to get a beer.

I stand in the shower for a few minutes. The water is like pins and needles, but I lather up, rinse the soap off, then turn off the water. I wrap the towel around me and run into my room. I grab a pair of pajamas and throw them on, then roll onto my bed. Maybe I can get a couple of hours of sleep.

"Jimmy...Jimmy, wake up. Oh, my God, Jimmy, what happened to you?"

"It's a long story, Ma," I say. "I gotta get to work."

I get into the bathroom, and put on my work clothes. I quickly run a comb through my hair, and discover I have a few cuts on my scalp, too. I brush my teeth and run down the stairs.

"Ma, I'm leaving! See you later!"

I have no idea how I'm going to make it through the work day.

CHAPTER 48

Bobby Comes Home

Barbara put Bobby into a cab at curbside and gave him her phone number. "I'm not home much, but if I can ever help you, let me know," she said.

He was grateful for the offer.

The cab driver, who had an accent surprisingly similar to Cesar's, dodged traffic from LaGuardia and pulled up in front of a plain, three-story gray building.

The sign over the door read "Sts. Agnes and Clare Residence."

Oh, great. I go from Brothers of Mercy to the home of some saints. I never went to Catholic school and never really paid attention in Catechism class.

Bobby sat in the back seat while the driver got his bags and wheelchair out of the trunk. He could feel his heart beating faster and faster. He had no idea what was waiting for him once he passed through the arch under the Sts. Agnes and Clare sign.

He put head in his hand and was thinking about what he could expect when the driver came back to his side of the cab.

"Hey, Bobby! We're so glad you made it!"

A woman he'd never seen before was next to the driver, all smiles, and holding the handles on Bobby's wheelchair.

"I got the brakes on, man. We're gonna put *chew* in this baby and give *chew* a ride to *chore* new pad. Rosemary here's got it all set up."

The driver and Rosemary reached in and worked together to transfer Bobby from the back seat onto the wheelchair. Rosemary gave the orders. The driver released the brakes and pushed the chair through the front door.

"I've got it from here, Jorge," Rosemary said.

"Jorge, thank you," Bobby said. He hadn't even bothered to see what his driver's name was. Now he reached into his shirt pocket and pulled out a ten-dollar bill.

"Here, take this. Appreciate your efforts on my behalf."

"*Chew* will be fine, fine," Jorge said. "Rosemary and the people who work here, they good people. I come here every now and then. I'll ask about you, bro. They got my number at the front desk. If *chew* need a cab, *chew* know who to call."

"Yeah, I do. Thanks, Jorge."

Rosemary waved goodbye to Jorge, and turned to Bobby.

"You have a studio apartment on the first floor," she told Bobby. "It's small, but it has wide doors and a walk-in shower, so it should make things easier for you. No stairs."

"Yeah, I kinda have problems with stairs," he said.

"You may want to cook for yourself...although there are some of the older women who work here who might want to do some cooking for you. Especially since you're Italian—you *are* Italian, right? We have some ladies who cook these massive Italian meals and have no one to feed them to. You will become a target for them with their culinary skills," she said.

"Could be a good thing, I guess," he said, realizing how hungry he was, as he thought about lasagna, meatballs, linguini and fettuccini.

They stopped in front of a door marked 117.

"This one is yours," Rosemary said. She leaned over and turned the key. She pushed him inside.

He couldn't believe what he saw: an apartment that looked as if it had been made just for him.

Straight ahead, he saw a couch under two very high windows. *It is the first floor, after all, in the city, so you can't have floor-to-ceiling windows.* To the left, he noticed a table that was low enough that he could just wheel himself over to it and eat without having to stretch at all.

The bathroom was on the right, back-to-back with a small closet. In front of the table was a small kitchen and refrigerator. He wheeled himself toward the kitchen sink and its low sink. The phone was mounted on the wall, but at wheelchair height. Even the small television was on a TV table that was shorter than in most living rooms.

"It's only a studio, so it's not as if you have a lot of room here, Bobby," Rosemary explained. "The couch is actually your bed. It's a futon that converts into a bed. We could also bring in an electrically controlled recliner, if you want one of those.

"Tomorrow, we'll have an aide come in and get everything set up for you. Groceries, pots and pans, towels, stuff like that. We tried to anticipate what you'd need, but I'm sure we forgot something.

"Do you want me to help you unpack, or do you want to just try to unwind for a while? I can leave you alone, or I can stay awhile. Your choice."

"I don't exactly know yet. Let me think."

"You get your bearings and let me know. I'm on the front desk until 11 tonight. You dial seven and then zero, and you'll get me on the phone," Rosemary said.

She started to leave, then asked, "Can you transfer yourself to bed?"

"No, I haven't quite mastered that yet."

"We'll get right to that tomorrow. In the meantime, I'll help you tonight. I'll stay on the desk until you feel like you're ready for bed. Call me, okay?"

She left.

He took a deep breath and inhaled the air, holding it in his lungs for as long as he could.

This is what my home smells like. My little corner of the world.

CHAPTER 49

Jenny Flirts with Bud

Jenny drove as Bud looked for 947 Walnut Street. Tom was following them in Bud's car.

From Jenny's point of view, any time spent with Bud was worth driving all the way from Georgia.

"Okay, here it is. Pull over and park."

"What's this person's name, again, Tom?"

"Cindy Bishop. She should be expecting us," Tom replied.

Jenny was reluctant to go up the walk. "Bud, I'm not sure I want to stay here," she said.

It turned out not to matter, since no one answered the door.

"Okay, now what?" Jenny asked.

"Well, we can't go back to the dorm, that's for sure," Bud finally said. "Let's see if there's a motel near campus. We can all stay there for tonight and then get a fresh start in the morning."

"Not me, man. I have a class at eight in the morning. I gotta get back to the dorm and sleep in my own bed," Tom said.

"Okay. You take my car back to campus and park it in that back lot. Jenny and I will try to find a motel, and then we'll be back on campus in the morning. Jenny, you okay with that?"

"Sure." Jenny was happy that things didn't work out with the elusive Cindy Bishop and that she would be headed to a motel with Bud. She was also glad Tom wouldn't be a third wheel when she and Bud would be in a motel together.

"Sayonara, kiddo," Tom said, as he headed for Bud's car, then took off.

They drove in silence until they saw a place called The Moonbird Motel.

Bud walked in to the front desk and rang the bell. A slightly disheveled clerk came out from the back room.

"Sir, I would like a room for the night. Do you have one with two beds? It's for my sister and me."

"Sure, sure. Okay." The clerk looked down at the register and said, "We only have one room with two beds. Forty dollars for the night. Room 107."

Bud reached into his pocket and pulled out two twenty-dollar bills. It was all the money he had left until next Wednesday.

"You can probably park right outside the room," the clerk drawled.

They parked, and Bud used the key to open the flimsy door to room 107.

There were two beds inside, but only about six inches separated them from each other. The end table had cigarette burns all over it, and the lamp-shade had a few, too. The room reeked of cigarette smoke and maybe even other types of smoke. He knew it would be difficult for him to get to sleep here, but he felt that he had no choice.

Bud sighed. "Jenny, you're sleeping in your clothes tonight."

"I have a blanket I use at the lake in my car. I'm going to get it and put it on top of the bedspread," she said. "This place is disgusting!"

She was right; the place *was* disgusting.

They went back into the room and Jenny put the blanket on top of the bed closest to the door. She sat on top of it and curled up.

"Bud," she said, "you can't sleep in that dirty bed. You have to come over here with me."

"No, Jenny, I'll sleep in the chair. Good night."

She couldn't believe it.

Was I an idiot to come all this way to see him, just because I have been in love with him since the sixth grade? Doesn't he know this?

She dozed off and on, as did Bud.

CHAPTER 50

Donut Shop Surprise

I get to the donut shop—facial cuts, shiner and all—exactly at 8 AM, keeping my eyes on the floor as I head back to unload boxes.

Al sees me.

"What the hell happened to you? You going for the middleweight championship of the world?"

"We were at the beach last night, and this guy picked a fight with me. I tried to walk away, but he decked me, so I hit him back, then it got worse. I don't really know how it ended. He knocked me out. I woke up on the beach, in the sand, and I was all wet."

"Did you know this guy?"

"Never saw him before last night. I think he knew Terry and Eddie, though."

"You gotta admit, Jimmy, those guys are not really the best company for you to keep."

"You sound like my dad, Al. He hates them."

"He may have good reason, Jim. They're known around town as a couple of bums. They attract bums like themselves."

"Well, Terry and Eddie were drunk as skunks when I got there, so I never got the guy's name. He had a pretty good right hook, though."

"That's what the eye is from?"

"Yeah. That was the first punch," I admit. "He had a couple of other guys with him. I didn't recognize them either."

"Well, enough of that. Let's get cracking on these boxes. And Jimmy, stay back here instead of going out front today."

I see I have enough to keep me busy, as he heads out to the counter.

But he returns to the back right away, followed by a Weymouth cop.

"Jimmy, this policeman wants to have a word with you."

"Are you James Bailey?" the cop asks me.

"Yes, sir, I am."

"What happened to your face? Were you in a fight recently?"

I explained that someone had thrown a punch at me, so I fought back to protect myself.

"I was at Wessagusset Beach with some of my friends," I say.

"That wouldn't happened to have been last night, was it, son?"

"Yes...yes, it was. Why?"

"We found a body on the beach. The guy was pretty messed up, like he had been in a fight. He face looked a lot like yours looks today. Do you know two guys named Eddie O'Donnell and Terence Bingham?"

"Yes, sir, I do."

"They have implicated you as having been there and pushed this guy into the water and watched him drown. Is that what happened?"

Pushed him into the water? Watched him drown? HE DROWNED?

"No, sir, that is not what I recall. I am telling the truth."

"We need you to come with us to the station for questioning. We have O'Donnell and Bingham at the station as well."

"The guy who drowned...Who was he? I had never seen him before last night."

"He is—was—from Southie. Name of Paulie Donovan. He had a record for petty crime—small robberies, walking out on food, taking beer from the packies, that kind of thing. Rumor also had it he was trying to get into the Winter Hill gang with Whitey Bulger, but that's just heresay. He was also a small-time boxer. He never did anything big. Like throwing someone in the water and watching him drown."

The cop reaches for his handcuffs to put them on me.

"You have the right to remain silent...Anything you say can and will be used against you in a court of law...You have the right to counsel..."

He's arresting me! He's giving me a Miranda warning! Oh, my God! I need a lawyer! What am I going to do now? I didn't kill anyone. I know I didn't.

Al is standing to one side with his mouth open. "Where are you taking him, officer? Isn't he entitled to a lawyer?"

"We're going to headquarters. You got a lawyer for him? Send the lawyer over."

"Al, call my mother!"

"Will do, Jimmy."

The cop pushes my head down into the back seat of the cruiser. My face is a bruised mess, it aches, my head hurts, and I'm sleep-deprived.

My whole world is swirling on a crooked axis.

CHAPTER 51

Learning to Live

Bobby rolled around the apartment, like a pinball from one corner to the other, trying to get his bearings.

He wished more natural light could come into this place. And he needed to get out more.

The doorbell rang. He wheeled over to open it.

"Mr. Mangino? I'm Lily, and I've been assigned to be your weekday aide. May I come in?"

"Sure," he replied.

He wheeled his chair in reverse, but only enough so that she could get through.

She was a light-skinned African-American woman, or maybe she was Hispanic. Bobby couldn't tell. He didn't want to ask. Maybe she would tell him about her heritage on her own. He didn't want to pry. But he thought it was ironic that she was named for a white flower and she had cafe-au-lait-colored skin. She was stunningly beautiful, he thought. She was carrying a clipboard and a black-and-white composition notebook. She wore a light blue uniform, with a name tag on the left side, under her shoulder.

"May I sit on the couch?" she asked.

"Sure," he replied. "What are we doing here?"

"Well, first off, my job is to find out what you need in the apartment. It's a nice apartment, isn't it?"

"It's a little small," he replied, "and I wish I could get some more natural light in here, but it's more than I expected, really."

"Ok, Bobby. I need to make a list of things you might need. Household items. Sheets, towels, pots, pans, drinking glasses, dishes, silverware, whatever you think you might need. Can you think of anything?"

"I need all of those things. I never had my own place before."

"I will get those things for you. And also, groceries. What do you want me to get for you in the grocery store? What kind of food do you like?"

"Let me think about that one for a few minutes. Do we have to do anything else while I think about that?"

"Yes. I have to go over a bunch of things with you. Are you able to do a self-transfer, from your wheelchair to a toilet, or from the chair to the bed?"

"No, I always had help with that. I was in a nursing home in Clarence, out in western New York, before I came back to the city. I was almost strong enough to do a transfer, but not quite."

"Well, we're going to work on that. You look pretty strong to me. You can't sleep in that chair!"

She showed him how to flip the futon feature of the couch flat and make it into a bed, and then flipped a lever to bring the couch up higher so that it was even with the height of Bobby's chair. "Bring yourself over here."

Bobby followed her directions. She demonstrated.

"But once I get onto the couch, how do I flip my legs further in so that they're not falling off?" he asked.

"That's what I'm going to show you next."

She went out into the hallway and brought in a cane with a hooked handle.

What the hell? Does she think I can walk? With a cane? That ain't happening!

"Once you get your tush on the bed, and you get the legs even down by the side of the bed, you should take this cane handle and flip one leg at a time, like this, onto the bed." She demonstrated how it would work. "It will take practice, and you won't get it on the first try. But you have strong arms. I can see them from here. You have to depend on your arms to help you.

"Then you do things in reverse to get back in the chair. But you have to remember to always put the brakes on your chair. Otherwise, you'll be on your butt on the floor and won't be able to do anything until I get here for my daily visit."

"You'll be coming every day?"

"Yup, Except on weekends or when I'm on vacation, then I'll send one of my friends from the agency.

"And at night you can always call whoever's on the front desk to help you get into bed, until you get the hang of this," Lily reminded him.

"I forgot about that," he said. "Yeah, Rosemary told me that. I forgot."

"And if you like baseball, I have a friend who works over at Shea Stadium. I think you'd like to meet him. He works for the Mets. My friend's name is Al Weis. He used to be an infielder for the Mets, but now he works in the office. I took care of his mother for a while."

"Really? For the Mets? I've never been to Shea. I've only been to Yankee Stadium in the Bronx."

She put the bed back into couch mode and showed him again how to convert it into a bed. "Now you do it," she said. "You will be tested on this later."

I bet I will.

CHAPTER 52

Busted

'm at the police station, handcuffed, being watched by the same sergeant who gave me my safety patrol certification when I went to the Seach School.

I'm not a criminal; I'm a baseball player, and in the off-season, I've been working as a lackey in the donut shop.

I defended myself against that guy. But I didn't kill him.

My body hurts. My face hurts. Every part of me hurts. Wish I had the guts to ask for an aspirin or something for the headache that's pounding in my brain. I don't dare ask for anything. I could also use a drink of water.

Al walks in with another man in a three-piece navy-blue suit. His hair is short, almost a military-style cut, and he's wearing a red-striped tie.

"Jimmy, this is Joel Goldblum. He's a friend of mine, a lawyer. You shouldn't talk to the cops without a lawyer," Al says.

"Pleased to meet you, Jimmy," Joel says, "May I sit down with you?"

"Al, did you call my mother?" I ask.

"Yes. I expect she'll be here soon."

Joel gets up and goes over to the sergeant. They talk for a few minutes and he returns to the bench.

"I asked for a private room, where we can talk," he explains. "I need to know what happened."

The cop who arrested me comes sauntering down the hallway and tells me to get up. "You want a room where you can talk to your client, Mr. Goldblum?"

The cop knows Joel by name. Is that a good sign or a bad one?

"Yes, Officer Gordon, that's what I've asked for. Anything available?"

"Yeah. Come with me." He looks over at me. I jump up as fast as I can.

He leads us to a small room with a rectangular table in the middle. Only four chairs will fit around the table. There is only one light, overhead, and it can't be more than a 40-watt bulb.

"Officer Gordon—how about taking the handcuffs off my client? He's not going anywhere."

"Mr. Goldblum, this is a *murder* case. You expect me to treat him in some special way?"

"No, I expect you to treat him like a human being. Take the handcuffs off, please. You can put them back on when we're done."

Gordon sighs, then reaches into his pocket and takes out a set of keys, stretches over to my side of the table and unlocks the handcuffs, and very quickly they snap open.

"Thank you, Officer Gordon. We'd like to be alone now," Joel says.

"So, Jimmy, let's start from the beginning. What exactly happened at the beach?"

I go through the details of how I went to the beach later than I had wanted to, that Terry and Eddie were blasted drunk when I got there, and that I had money to give them for my share of the beer, but this guy...this Paulie...wouldn't give me a beer, then we started fighting and ended up in the water, and how I passed out, because I think he hit me pretty hard, and woke up in the water with sand all over me.

"So you are saying it was self-defense?"

"Well, that guy hit me first," I say. "I was defending myself. All I wanted was a beer. I was willing to pay for it."

"Who bought the booze? Did you get it by using a fake ID?"

"No. Terry and Eddie always bought it. I just usually threw in some money to help pay for it. I don't know how they got it."

"And you say you never saw the deceased before last night, when he hit you first?"

"Never. And I was completely sober when I got there. It was dark. There were a couple others there I'd never seen, but they I never got a good look at their faces."

Joel pulls out a yellow legal pad and writes.

"Have you made a statement to the police yet?"

"No, Al told me to wait for my lawyer."

"Al gave you good advice," Joel says. "They'll be in here in a few minutes, and you will have to talk to them. Just follow my lead when then ask questions. Understand?"

"Yeah, I got it. Joel...You got any Tylenol?"

"No, but I can probably get some for you. You need anything else?"

"Yeah. Water please."

"You're gonna need both, once Detective Morris gets here," Joel says. "They're going to put you through the ringer. Just pay attention to me, Jimmy. Don't think about your family, your friends, your baseball career. Just think about the situation from last night and look at me for advice. This is the most important thing you've dealt with in your life."

In my life.

Oh, how I wish I were facing The Cuban in a tied game with the bases loaded and no outs instead.

CHAPTER 53

The Mets

After weeks of practicing, Lily was satisfied that Bobby could make his own transfers from the wheelchair to the bed. She noticed his arms had gotten stronger, and she told him.

"Yeah, I'm almost up to where I was when I was getting ready to play ball," he said.

He put his chin on his hand, elbow on the wheelchair.

"God, I miss baseball."

"What a coincidence," she said. "Today we're going on a field trip to Shea Stadium."

"But there's no baseball going on now. It's the end of October."

"We're going to see my friend Al Weis. He wants to meet you. He said to bring you by, and today would be a good day. So let's get cracking."

As he went to grab his Montreal Expos hat, she grabbed it from him and said, "Oh, no you don't!" She reached into her bag and pulled out a brand new Mets hat and put it on his head.

"You gotta wear *this* one," she insisted. "You'll look great in orange and blue."

"So you want me to fit in at Shea Stadium? I guess I'll do it—for you."

"No, you'll do it for yourself. You look great."

As they got closer, Shea Stadium looked like the Coliseum in Rome to Bobby. He was impressed. He wondered if the field inside would be as impressive and impeccable as Yankee Stadium's.

When they arrived at the "Employees Only" entrance, Lily parked Bobby in his wheelchair off to one side and then picked up the telephone posted by the door. "Yes? This is Lily...Yes...Al Weis is expecting us...Okay...We will wait here for him..."

The door opened, and out came Al Weis, a wiry guy about six feet tall. He had played shortstop and second base in his day. The Mets were the last team he played for during his ten years as a major leaguer.

Al hugged Lily and thanked her for coming. He headed over to Bobby and shook his hand. "Mr. Mangino, I've been waiting to meet you!"

"Mr. Weis, it is my honor to meet you," Bobby replied.

"Call me Al," he said.

"Yeah, and please, call me Bobby." They both laughed.

"Come on in and meet some of the people who work here," Al said.

Lily pushed the wheelchair through the door, where other Mets employees were waiting, sitting in a circle, to meet Bobby and Lily. Al was the only former player; the others had jobs like statistician and radio announcer. They reminisced about the '69 Mets, and gossiped about other teams.

"So, Bobby, the reason we wanted you to come here today is because we'd like to offer you a job."

They want me to work here? Doing what?

"We need someone here who can work with the scouting team to handle their reports. You'd be based here, and help the management team when they're getting ready for the draft," Al explained.

"What do you say, Bobby? Are you in?"

"I'm SO in!" Bobby said.

"When can you start?" Al asked.

"How about tomorrow?" Bobby replied.

"How about next Monday?" Al countered.

"You're on!" Bobby said.

Lily stood in the corner. She had worked on this, to get Bobby out of his apartment and back into baseball.

It was his life, and he needed to get back to it.

On the way back to the apartment, Lily told Bobby that she'd come early every morning to help him get to work.

Oh, my God! I will do anything we need to do to make this work. I'll be working for The Mets. I better read up on the team.

"Lily, can you get me a book on The Mets, like the 1969 Mets? I need to learn more about them," he said.

"I have so many books about the Mets, you can take your pick!"

Damn. I do look good in orange and blue.

CHAPTER 54

True Confessions

"Bud, the girl's in love with you. Are you that blind that you can't see that?" Tom wondered.

"I guess you're right, but I don't have time for that right now."

Jenny returned to their room.

"Well, my car's all packed. Guess I'll be heading home."

"Okay, I'll walk you to your car," Bud said.

The pay phone in the hallway rang.

"PRESCOTT! PHONE FOR YOU!"

When Bud answered, an unfamiliar female voice with a Boston accent was on the other end.

"This is Debbie Bailey. Jimmy's sister?"

"Hey, how are you, Debbie? I've heard a lot about you."

"Jimmy's in trouble. Bad trouble. He asked me to call you. He's in jail. For manslaughter."

"Manslaughter? He couldn't kill anyone! What happened?"

Debbie told him the entire story, as she knew it.

"Bud, he's so depressed and upset. But, I believe him. I don't think he could kill anyone, either."

Bud was speechless.

"What can I do, Debbie? I'm way down here in Nashville. I can't leave right now."

"If you could just send him a letter in jail, I think it would mean the world to him," she said. "I think if he heard from you, it would make a difference. He talks about you all the time."

"Send it to him, in care of Old Colony Correctional Center, One Administration Road, Bridgewater, Massachusetts 02324. They're evaluating him to see if he's psychologically capable to stand trial."

Psychologically capable of standing trial? Why wouldn't he be? He's got to be innocent.

"Debbie...Why wouldn't he be capable of standing trial"

"Bud, he's been through a lot since that night. The cops, the press, have put him through the ringer, and our Dad..."

Oh, yeah, your Dad...He was always worried about upsetting his Dad, not being the best for his Dad, not living up to his Dad's standards.

"Our whole family is a mess. My mother spends most of the day crying. My sister Donna is with her now. Donna had to come home. Both of us are up to our necks, between this and school. The press is skewering him, too. Going after him by interviewing people he went to high school with, making things up.

"If you could write him a letter, it will mean so much to him. I mean it. And if you can get any of the other players to write to him, I know it would help.

"He's on suicide watch right now at the prison."

"Suicide watch? He couldn't kill himself, either. Yeah, I can write to him, tonight or tomorrow."

"Thanks. I'll keep you posted," she said, "now that I know how to find you."

Bud returned the receiver to the phone. He went back to his room. The color was completely gone from his face.

"Whoa, what's happened to you? Did someone die?" Tom asked.

"As a matter of fact, someone did, and my friend from the Falcons is being accused of manslaughter in his death."

"What? Oh, man, it was just a joke, Bud. I'm sorry. Who?"

"Jimmy...Jimmy Bailey. Another pitcher. From Boston. Long story. That was his sister, calling to tell me that Jimmy's in jail, under observation, under suicide watch. They're trying to figure out if he's psychologically fit to stand trial in this guy's death. They found the guy dead in the ocean after he and Jimmy had a fight on the beach."

"Oh, wow! What did she want you to do? You can't go up there. You got too much to do here."

"She wants me to write him a letter in prison. She says he'd really appreciate hearing from me and some of the other guys from the team. This hits me straight in the gut."

Tom spoke up. "Well, Jenny, it's about time you hit the road, right? You can get pretty close to home before it gets dark if you leave now."

They arrived at her car and she got in. Bud leaned down and gave her a hug. "Drive safely," he cautioned.

Tom then leaned in and gave Jenny a hug that lasted longer than Bud's had. Tom even kissed Jenny on the head before she closed the door. "Take care of yourself, little Miss Murphy," Tom said. "Let us know when you get home."

She pulled away, waving as she drove down the driveway.

"Nice girl," Tom said. "I like her."

"I see that," Bud replied.

"You got a problem with that?"

"Not at all. I've got a letter to write."

I need to call the guys and get them to write him, too. Skip and Cesar, too. Russ. I know he needs to hear from Russ. I should try to track Bobby down. Wonder what he's doing in New York City. I need to call home. I need to talk to Mama and Daddy about this. These are the times when I need my grandmother. She would know exactly what to do.

CHAPTER 55

Bridgewater State Prison

They tell me I'm on suicide watch. I have no intention of killing myself. I want to go to trial and show them I'm innocent.

No TV here. No radio. Newspapers and magazines, but they're old ones. The noise is outrageous. I can't sleep more than a couple of hours every night.

I get visits from my lawyer. He seems like a pretty good guy. He asks good questions. I try to focus enough to answer him. I tell him the truth every time he asks me about that night. I have not changed my story. Not one bit. It's the truth. Why would I change the truth?

The district attorney from Norfolk County, though: I hate him. He twists my words every time, and Joel has to stop him with, "That is not what my client said, and you know it, Steve. We've been over and over this."

Joel seems to trust me.

Terry and Eddie, who were drunk when this all went down, and said that I pummeled that guy and threw him in the water. I don't think they *know* what happened. Friends don't lie about their friends.

"Bailey? "Mail for you." The guard flips an envelope into my cell and walks away.

The letter is postmarked: Nashville. I rip it open.

It's from Bud. I can't believe it.

Dear Jimmy: I heard from your sister Debbie that you are in prison, await-ing a trial for something you didn't do. I know you didn't do what you have been accused of, because I know you aren't capable of doing that.

I spoke to my parents, and they said you should make sure you have a good lawyer. If you don't feel that you have one, my Dad said he knows someone in Boston who might be able to help you. Dad says that a good lawyer is crucial when it comes to fighting charges like this.

As for me, I am studying hard in school, and I have to tell you, it's a lot harder than I thought it was going to be. I am in the pre-med classes, and it's a lot of work. I have six or seven hours of homework every night, plus lots of work on weekends.

I have not been very good about keeping in touch with many of the guys on the team. I know that Bobby moved back to New York City a few weeks ago. Some lady from Clarence, New York helped him to find an apartment for handicapped people near Shea Stadium, so he went over there and applied for a job. He got a job with The Mets! Isn't that incredible?

I have a roommate from Maryland, and he has apparently fallen for a woman from my home town who recently came up here to see me.

If there is any way that I can get up there to see you, I will. I hope you will write me back.

Your friend,

Bud

My friend, Bud.

Yes, Bud, you are my friend.

You're the real deal.

The peacemaker.

The leader.

My friend.

CHAPTER 56

Dr. Beacon

Every time they send the psychiatrist to see me, I can't figure out what he expects to hear.

Dr. Beacon is an odd little man, who wears brown tweed sport coats with rust-colored suede patches on the elbows. Under the sport coat, he wears polo shirts, wrinkled khaki pants and usually brown socks with worn-out loafers. Some days he combs his sand-streaked brown hair, some days not, so it's often wild, kind of like the old photos I remember of Einstein.

When he comes to speak to me, he asks the guard to take us to a small conference room so that "we can talk."

Dr. Beacon says he must give me many tests to determine whether I can withstand the rigors of a trial. He tells me again and again that they have already indicted me.

Then I say I'm not guilty, that I did not kill Paulie Donovan, that I was just defending myself.

He looks me up and down, as I sit with my elbows on the table.

"Jimmy, what you are saying to me is what every indicted inmate tells me. Do you recall becoming enraged when the man came after you? Is that what caused his death?"

"Are you asking if he made me mad when he punched me?"

"Yes, I am trying to find out what your feelings were on that night."

"I was mad because he wouldn't give me a beer. I had money to pay for it, but he wouldn't take my money. He was taunting me so I took the beer. He came after me. Terry and Eddie were drunk and they wouldn't stick up for me. I was on my own with that guy. He started hitting me so I hit him back. We ended up in the water, rolling around, hitting each other, and then he hit me really hard, and I woke up, covered in sea water and sand, on the beach. That's what I've told you, time and time again, and I told the police the same thing, time and time again."

"How did that make you feel, when you woke up, covered in sea water and sand?" Dr. Beacon asks. "Were you angry? Were you enraged? Were you looking for revenge?"

"I didn't know what to think or feel," I reply. "In fact, I couldn't feel anything except pain from where he hit me. I pulled myself up and started to walk home. It's about a mile. Someone stopped and gave me a ride. I got cleaned up, then I went to work. I had no idea he was dead."

"Really? Even after you killed him by throwing him into the ocean?"

"I told you, I never threw him into the ocean! We were rolling in the ocean and fighting," I say. "As far as I knew, when I woke up, he had walked away and was on his way home, too.

"And now, my father has given up on me, my mother is devastated, my sisters are shocked, and all I can think of is that I will never see the outside, or be in a baseball field again. I'll never see my coaches or play under the lights.

"My life is nothing but a big bank of empty seats."

The tables turn. I watch him, in silence, in the same way a hawk might look at dinner prey for almost five minutes. I have no thoughts of hurting him in the way a hawk might be considering doing to a smaller bird that might be his next meal; I'm just trying to figure out what is going on in his brain. What, exactly, do psychiatrists think, anyway? How do they know who's pulling their leg or who is sincere? By looking at blobs of ink on a page?

He looks up and realizes that I am studying him, and seems stunned. He jumps slightly in his seat and asks, "What? What are you thinking?"

"I am thinking about ink blobs," I respond.

"Ink BLOTS," he corrects me.

"To you, they're blots, to me, they're blobs," I say.

"Don't be so sarcastic," he says. "It doesn't become you."

"What *does* become me, Dr. Beacon? What would get me out of here?"

"An innocent verdict during a *bona fide* trial," he replies. "A trial before a jury of your peers."

A jury of my peers? You mean like Terry and Eddie? Or like Bud and Bobby? Or like Debbie and Donna?

"So that's how things work, huh? That's what makes the legal system fair, right?"

He stares at me silently.

CHAPTER 57

Yogi Answers the Door

Lily helped Bobby get ready for his second day of working for the Mets. He had no idea what this job might become.

"Um, um, Bobby, you spend more time on your hair than anybody I know!" she said.

Lily put his Mets hat on the door handle so he wouldn't forget it on the way out the door. He headed down to the front desk, where Rosemary said his cab had arrived.

Bobby gave the driver a few instructions, and the two of them got Bobby into the chair.

Bobby was proud of himself: he had just taught someone how to do a transfer. This was the first time only two of them got him into his chair from a car.

He wheeled himself to the employees' door and rang the bell. The man who opened the door looked familiar to him.

I know that face, I know I do.

Yogi Berra.

"Hey, you're our new guy, right?" Yogi said. "Man-GEE-no, right? I heard about you from Cesar Dominguez. He says you're all right."

*I was never "all right" with Cesar. In fact, I was pretty much of an ass to Cesar. Wow. And he gave me a reference with Yogi Berra. **THE** YOGI BERRA.*

"Pleased to meet you, Mr. Berra," Bobby said.

"Yogi, call me Yogi," he said. "Come on in, we've got work to do."

Bobby looked at the lines on Yogi's face.

How many stories are in that face? How many Buds and Jimmys and Bobbys has he known in his time? I wonder if he's ever seen a baseball prospect show up in a wheelchair.

"So Bobby, I see that thing doesn't slow you down. You move pretty good in that. We can use someone who's as quick as you," Yogi said.

"I was faster when I played, up in Jamestown."

"Jamestown? Home of Lucille Ball? I been there. Good baseball gets played up there."

"I was a pitcher, reliever, Yogi. Wish you could have been my catcher!"

"It would be my honor someday to take a throw from you," Yogi said. "But now, we're going to meet with the scouting staff. We might be putting you in that department."

Scouting? They might want me to go on the road and look for talent? Wow. How great would that be?

"Wherever you want me to work, Yogi, I'm there. I'm just so happy to be working for The Mets. Period. Yup. Yup. Yup."

CHAPTER 58

Lost in Space

I wasn't crazy when I came to this place, but I feel like I might be now.

I long for the scent of newly-mown grass on a pristine baseball field. I yearn for one full minute of silence, so I might be able to think about my future.

No light shines in here, unless it's artificial.

No silence in this place. Not even for a second. Noise steps over each sound until it becomes a roar, an unending racket that blasts through my brain.

My father won't visit me; when my mother comes, she cries the entire time while I'm speaking to her over the prison phone. Debbie comes and talks for a few minutes and simply asks if the food is okay. I tell her it's horrible, and she says she will see what she can do. I've received a letter from Donna, but she didn't say anything hopeful.

I cherish Bud's words. I frequently remove the letter from the envelope and read it over and over again. I wish I could see him and sit with him and just talk to him for five minutes.

Visiting hours are coming up.

"Bailey? You got a visitor. I think you want to see him," the guard says, and he takes me out to the phones.

I sit down in a cubicle, not knowing what to expect. I pick up the phone.

"Jimmy," the voice at the other end says. "You don't know me, but I know you. I heard you're a good pitcher, you got good command on the mound."

"I don't recognize you," I reply. "Who are you?"

"Bill Lee, from the Red Sox," he says. "You know, The Spaceman. I heard you need someone to talk to. You hang in there, kid."

Bill Lee? Left-handed pitcher for my Red Sox?

"I read about you in the newspaper," he says. "I think you're being framed. I talked to your lawyer, and I told him I'd come give you a pep talk. I don't have a lotta time, but I just wanna let you know I'm thinkin' about you. A lot of the guys on the pitching staff are."

"They are?"

"Yeah, they are. We're all pitchers, ain't we? So you just stay strong, and I'll try to get back here to see ya when we get back from our next road trip, ya hear?"

"Yes, I understand," I reply. "I'm doing the best I can."

"Can't ask for more than that. See ya later, son."

He hangs up the phone and gives me kind of a half salute and a half smile, then stands up and walks away. He looks ten feet tall.

I'm still seated for a few seconds before I hang up the phone on my side of the Plexiglas partition. I stand up and the guard comes over to return me to my cell.

That was really Bill Lee. He came to see me and tell me to hang in. He said he thinks I'm being framed. I can't wait to tell Joel. Maybe he can find some proof. Maybe I can get out of this godforsaken place.

CHAPTER 59

Joel's Advice

keep reliving the discussion I had last week with Bill Lee.

I hear big boots coming down the hallway. Sometimes it's hard to hear the *thud, thud, thud* with all the other noise around here. They stop in front of my cell.

"Bailey, you got a visitor. No ballplayer this time. Your lawyer. Let's go."

"Yeah. Okay."

He opens the cell door, grabs me by the elbow and walks me past two other cells. Their occupants shout random obscenities. We walk to the big door, and it opens electronically.

We go to one of the small conference rooms where lawyers and inmates can meet. Joel is waiting for me.

"You got 30 minutes from now," the guard says. "I'll be timing you."

"Hey, Jimmy, how are you holding up? I hear you had a celebrity visitor last week."

"Yeah, Bill Lee came to see me," I say.

"Nice gesture," Joel says. "Let's get to work."

"Jimmy, I hate to say this, but there is mounting evidence that you pushed Paulie Donovan into the water," Joel says.

"What do you mean?" I ask.

"Terry and Eddie are standing by their story that it was you, and you alone, fighting in the water with Paulie. They signed affidavits and turned them over to the district attorney."

"But Joel, Terry and Eddie were so drunk they couldn't even speak. How would they know what happened?"

"That's what you've been saying all along," Joel says, as he writes a few notes onto his yellow pad.

"I believe you, but, God, Jimmy, we've got to get some proof. You have no idea who the other guys were? None at all? And Terry and Eddie wouldn't know, either?"

"You would have to ask them," I reply.

Joel scribbles again, looking down at the yellow pad.

"Jimmy...I have a detective working the beach, to see if there are any people who live close to the beach who might have seen anything that night. So far, no one remembers anything from that night."

"There's a bunch of people who go down the beach every night to get high," I say. "They live around the area—Bradley Road, North Street, Sea Street. Maybe one of them saw something," I say.

"I'll have the detective check that, too," Joel says.

He makes another note on his legal pad.

"It'll probably be hard to convince any of them to testify on your behalf, since what they're doing at the beach most of the time is illegal. They hide behind the bath house and drink, do drugs, that kinda thing."

Once again, Joel is right.

"What the hell am I going to do? My career is over, my father won't speak to me, my mother cries all the time, and I haven't even gotten to the preliminary hearing. I don't know how I'll pay you."

"That's the least of your worries," Joel says. "We have a lot of work to do."

"THIRTY MINUTES! TIME'S UP!"

"Jimmy, try to remember what those guys looked like, if you can. It could be helpful as I send my detectives over to Southie."

CHAPTER 60

Mom Visits Bobby

"So, Bobby, your little place is cute," his mother said. "A little small, but cute."

"It kinda has to be small, Ma, because things have to stay within reach," Bobby replied. "I've gotta be able to pull down the couch and get into it as a bed and then get out of it every day to get ready for work. It's really pretty handy, all things considered."

"Oh, you sound pretty high and mighty there, 'all things considered.' Where'd you go to college? Do we have to start calling you 'Dr. Robert Mangino, Jr.,' doctor of baseball?"

"C'mon, Ma, I have to wear a tie to work now, so I need to speak properly," he said. "I get up every morning, my aide comes in to help me get cleaned up, shaved, ready to go, and then I call a cab and take it to work."

"You pay for a cab? Are you serious?"

"Yeah, the Mets actually pay for it," he said.

"And Ma, I've been working with Yogi Berra."

"Yogi??? Oh, my God, Bobby? Yogi?? I love Yogi! Do you think you might be able to introduce me to him some day?"

"Some day, maybe. Okay, Ma?"

"Sure. But I can't wear a Mets hat, Bobby, honest, I can't."

He laughed. "Don't worry, I won't ask you to."

"Bobby, why didn't you try to get a job with the Yankees?"

"Ma, we been over this time and time again. I can't get to Yankee Stadium, even in a cab, in less than an hour. Flushing to the Bronx? Traffic is nuts. Going from this apartment to Shea is enough for me."

"I guess."

"I had something else I wanted to tell you, though, Ma. You know I had a coupla friends in Jamestown I played ball with? Bud from Georgia and Jimmy from Boston?"

"Yeah, you mentioned them to me."

"Well, Jimmy got arrested and he's been charged with manslaughter. He got into a fight with some guy at the beach and the guy drowned."

"Oh, my God, Bobby! Did he do it?"

"Not if what he's told me is true. Jimmy says the guy threw the first punch and he just defended himself, but I'm worried about him, Ma. His dad won't even speak to him."

"Has his mother abandoned him, too, Bobby?"

"No, but all she does is cry when she goes to see him, Ma."

"I'd probably cry all the time if my Bobby was in jail."

"I owe him a letter," Bobby said. "He sent me a long one, and I haven't answered yet."

"Could you go to see him?" she asked.

"I don't think so. But I can write to him."

CHAPTER 61

Letter from the Mets

"Bailey! Who you know at the New York Mets?"

The guard throws a letter into my cell.

"I dunno."

The New York Mets?

I open the envelope with the orange-and-blue logo as its return address.

Dear Jimmy,

I heard from Bud that you were arrested and that you are in jail. I don't know what to say. I've never been in jail, but I know a lot of guys I went to school with who have. I've never been inside a jail cell. It must be awful.

As you know, I was in a bus accident on my way back home after the end of the season. I was hurt real bad and now can't move my legs. I'm in a wheelchair. I get around pretty good. They got me an apartment made for people in wheelchairs. As my mom says, it's small, but it works for me. I have an aide who comes in every morning and helps me get ready for the day.

You see I'm sending you a letter on New York Mets stationery. I got a job with the Mets, thanks to the people at this housing place where I live, and my aide. They knew someone at the Mets, and the Mets found some work for me. I met Yogi Berra. He's the manager for the Mets now. He's been very nice to me so far, so I hope I don't disappoint him. I take a cab to work every day.

That was nice that Bill Lee from the Red Sox came by to see you. I wish there was some way I could come to see you, but now that I'm in this chair, it makes my life harder than it was before the accident.

If that changes, I'll be there.

Your friend,

Bobby

He has his freedom; I'm locked up.

CHAPTER 62

Freshman Year Ends

Bud can't believe he got through his first year at Vanderbilt, or that he made the dean's list both semesters.

He was ready to return to Jamestown or to an AA team.

But even better, the Expos were sending him to their AAA affiliate in Memphis instead. It was a big jump.

Tom, on the other hand, had a 2.7 average–a C-plus—so he needed to work harder next year.

Tom and Jenny had become an item. Jenny had moved to Nashville and gotten a job as a secretary at one of the record companies. Tom was a little nervous that she might meet a new guy there.

Jenny was 19 now, almost 20, and she lived with three other girls in a small apartment near the Grand Ole Opry.

She liked Charlie Pride and Loretta Lynn, because they reminded her of home, and she was homesick. But she had Tom.

Sometimes she'd hang out with Bud and talk about their high school friends.

Bud wasn't much for reminiscing, though. He wanted to move forward, not backward, and he had one goal: making it to the major leagues. He called it "The Show."

Tom came over all the time, and the roommates liked to cook meals for him and bake him cookies.

Bud dropped Tom off at Jenny's front door one evening. His car was loaded up like it was on the day he first arrived at school.

Jenny came out to greet them, and Bud said he was leaving that night.

"Where you going?"

"They're moving me up to AAA ball," he replied. "I'm going to Memphis to play for the Blues—still with the Expos, but a lot higher up in the organization. It's kinda like skipping a grade in school."

"Memphis? I think my dad knows some people there," she said.

"I'm going to take a little time and look at the country between here and Memphis," he told her. "Things are different in west Tennessee, I hear. It's more like Mississippi. I hear the music out there's pretty interesting, too."

She moved over toward him and gave him a full-body hug.

"Drive carefully, Bud." She hesitated for a couple of seconds. "And thanks for introducing me to Tom."

"Yeah. Be good to him, Jenny. He's an upright guy. Don't wanna see him get hurt."

"I would never hurt him, Bud. I never would've met him if it hadn't been for you."

Should I have let my guard down and just stayed with the home girl?

Not now. I need to focus.

This is not the time.

Stick with plan A.

CHAPTER 63

Bobby on the Road

June 24, 1974—Bobby's twenty-second birthday.

Bobby felt good working in the Mets organization.

He was on time for work every day, got along with everyone he met, people who loved the game as much he did.

He thought people at Sts. Agnes and Clare might rustle up a birthday cake for him. He had no idea the Mets had a much better gift in mind.

"Bobby, we need to talk to you," Lenny DaCosta said, with a solemn face. Lenny was the head of scouting operations for the Mets.

"Can we come in?" Al Weis and Yogi were with him, along with a couple of others he didn't recognize.

"Sure, come on in," Bobby said, although he only had a cubicle big enough to accommodate his wheelchair and his desk.

They crowded in around Bobby and his chair.

"We've figured out what we want you to do, going forward," Al said. "Lenny and his team need a new scout, so that's where you're going–on the road with the scouting team."

Bobby was speechless.

How will I be inconspicuous when I'm there to evaluate?

"Are you sure? I mean, the logistics."

"Don't worry about that, kid," Yogi said. "We'll figure it out."

"You'll start by shadowing one of the older guys," Lenny said. "We'll figure all the travel stuff out. The older guys can show you what we look for. Your specialty will be pitchers. Whad'ya think?"

"If you think I can do it, I'm game," Bobby replied. "What a great birthday present this is!"

"Oh, it's your birthday?" Al asked. "We didn't know!"

Next came a group of Mets employees with a cake, swarming the cubicle, singing "Happy birthday," telling him to blow out the candles and make a wish.

Make a wish? What more can I wish for? I'm back in baseball, without my legs. I hope I don't cry.

CHAPTER 64

Innocent Until Proven Guilty?

The guard walks me into the room where Joel is waiting.

For the first time since we met, Joel's calm attitude is missing.

He talks fast.

"Sit down, Jimmy. I'll tell you right up front, I'm not happy today."

I plop myself into the steel chair.

"We have to go to trial with what we've got, Jimmy," Joel says, "and we don't have much. We don't have any witnesses to corroborate your story. I can't get Terry or Eddie to change their stories. I can't get anyone who lives near the beach to say they saw what happened. I can't find the other guys you say were there with Donovan."

"You mean, they say I'm guilty, so I am? This is bullshit!"

I pick up the chair and throw it across the room.

I punch the wall with what used to be my pitching hand.

"They've offered you a plea deal, Jimmy," Joel says.

"No deal!" I scream. "I didn't do anything except defend myself against a guy who hit me! You've taken all the money I had in the world, and you can't find a way to defend me?"

"Jimmy, this isn't about me. It's about the system, it's about how the law works. If we can't find witnesses, here's what we've got. You were fighting with the guy in the water at the beach. The police find the guy dead in the ocean. The ocean is next to the beach. He's been punched a few times in the face, and he has other bruises on his body, indicating he'd been in a fight. You had bruises all over your body and face. You were the last person seen with him. Even if Terry and Eddie were drunk, they saw you fighting with him.

"Then some people did see you staggering down North Street, covered in sand, with wet clothes. You had blood coming from your nose and a bruise over your eye. That's what we've got."

All my life I'd been told that a person was innocent until proven guilty. Now my lawyer is telling me that I've been proven guilty, even before i stepped into a court room, even before I met a judge, even before anyone sat in a jury box?

"Joel, how the hell can this be happening? I mean, this is not the way it's supposed to work."

"The district attorney is really pushing here, Jimmy. I am doing the best I can. Al is trying to raise some money to help pay for further legal fees. Your sister has been talking to some people, too. I'm doing most of this work *pro bono*, so don't worry about the money."

"What does Dr. Beacon say? Am I crazy, or what?"

"His report isn't in yet. If he thought you were completely ready to stand trial, you would have been transferred out of here by now," Joel says.

"Is that a good or a bad sign?" I ask.

"I can't tell—yet," he replies. "It could go either way. I can't read him at all."

"So...Where do we go from here?"

"I'll be back next week. In the meantime, although I want you to remain hopeful, I don't know if I can find another direction to take this case in. I'm going to call one of my law professors at Suffolk to see if he can think of any new avenues for this case. Maybe he'll have some ideas."

No one believes me.

No one has faith in me.

How did this happen?

CHAPTER 65

Memphis Blues

The Memphis humidity drops down on Bud like heavy cotton candy melting at a county fair.

Putting on long pants is a test; peeling them off at the end of a workout is even harder. He thought Georgia was hot and humid. He'd never felt anything like Delta heat. Some of his teammates were from way north, and they were fainting after even the most minor workout.

At least I have some hot south experience. Some of these guys will take a long time to get acclimated. It's what grandma used to call an "angry oven heat."

He had a whole new team to meet, a new coaching staff, and new clubhouse guys to get to know.

Pitching coach for the Memphis Blues was Arnie McManus, a laid-back, tobacco-chewing North Carolinian who had once pitched for the Minnesota Twins. His old friend Harmon Killebrew dropped in to see Arnie from time to time when he was in town.

The manager, Cole Barry, was a former catcher for the New York Yankees, and he would love what you did one minute and scream at you about it the next. The players and coaching staff cringed at his unpredictable behavior.

Cole was originally from Mamaroneck, a town in Westchester County, just outside of New York City. The place was known more for expensive homes and exorbitant taxes than for sports.

His reputation when he was with the Yankees was that he could catch both ends of a doubleheader and then go out dancing with his wife later that night. Yankee pitchers loved him; he was known for throwing runners out when they were trying to steal, and for his shrewd knowledge of the game.

In some ways, Bud thought, Cole would have been a perfect pitching coach, knowing as he did exactly how to handle pitchers when he had been behind the plate.

Well, he may know a lot about baseball, but he's just weird. He doesn't seem to know much about managing people. I can't let him ruffle me. No. No way. Gotta stay cool. Both mentally and physically.

Maybe Cole is trying to show us how to deal with the heat we're going to feel when we step into Major League ballparks. Lots of crazies up there, I guess.

"Hey, Prescott!" one of the clubhouse guys came into the locker room. "Got a piece of mail for you!"

It was from Jimmy.

Hey Bud:

Things aren't going too good here. I met with my lawyer this morning. He says we don't have many options. The two guys I know, Terry and Eddie, who were there on that night, are still saying that they saw me fight with the dead guy on the beach. My lawyer says he has had a couple of detectives looking for the other guys who were there. I don't know who they are, so I can't even describe them. Without them, my lawyer thinks I'm doomed.

I guess I'm headed to prison. My lawyer is saying I should take a plea deal. I've spent all my bonus money paying this guy. I still owe him more. My sister Debbie is getting some donations from her friends at Harvard and some in the hometown, but I don't know how far that will go.

My mother still only cries when she comes in to see me. It's an awful scene. My father won't come in at all. My sister Donna is back down in your home area, in Georgia, going to nursing school, so I don't see her much. Debbie is in grad school, so she only comes when she can. I think I already told you that I got a visit from a Red Sox pitcher—Bill Lee.

Just one favor, Bud, if you could. Please send me a letter back. It means so much when I get a piece of mail.

Of course, I would love it if you could come in person some time, but I don't expect that you will.

Thank you, Bud. I hope your baseball career is going great. I know you're going to make it to the majors.

Your friend,

Jimmy

Jimmy's going to prison? He told me he didn't commit murder or man-slaughter, or whatever they're accusing him of, and I believe him.

Arnie walked in.

"Hey, Prescott, what gives?"

"Well, this guy I used to pitch with in Jamestown...he's sitting in a jail in Massachusetts. He's been arrested for manslaughter, and his lawyer says there's nothing they can do for him, that they can't find the witnesses that could possibly prove that my friend didn't do it."

"I know a coupla guys on the Red Sox," Arnie said. "Maybe I can call them and ask them to check it out."

"The problem is, the two witnesses they have, who were supposed to be Jimmy's friends, were drunk out of their minds, and they can't find the other guys who were on the scene. No one seems to know who they are."

"I don't want this eating at you when I need you to pitch. Know what I mean?"

Yeah, I know what you mean. This game's 95 percent mental, five percent physical, on most days. Except in this heat and humidity.

I want to make it to The Show.

"I want to pitch for you 150 percent, Arnie. I think you know that. But this thing with Jimmy...It's in the back of my mind...And my other friend from Jamestown, Bobby..."

"Mangino? Yeah, guess what? He's going on the road with an old friend of mine from Cincinnati, Billy Logan. Crazy guy. Lots of fun. Billy's going to turn Bobby into a scout—if your friend's willing to learn."

Bud laughed at that. Bobby, willing to learn?

"Seems like he's mellowed a little since he lost his legs. Baseball's the only thing he knows. Hope your friend Billy is ready for a project."

"He'll probably be just fine. Logan's son's in a wheelchair, so he's probably the best one on the Mets' scouting staff to go on the road with Bobby. Billy's son Jack and a bunch of his college friends were messin' around, drinkin' and all, when they were on spring break, and they all dared each other to dive into the water off these cliffs, and Jack snapped his spinal cord. He was a basketball player—All-American—in kinda the same situation as Bobby. He ended up goin' to law school. Now he negotiates contracts for athletes."

"Whoa. Well, Bobby never went to college."

"Tell me your friend's name again, the one in jail?"

"Bailey. Jimmy Bailey."

"Did his dad play ball? Seems I knew a Jimmy Bailey who was in the Cardinals organization, right after the war. Any relation?"

"Yeah. It's his dad."

"Never knew why he left professional baseball," Arnie said, shaking his head. "He was good. Damned good. Then he just dropped out of sight."

Out of sight. That about summed it up. Mrs. Pin-Up Girl called the shots. No more baseball for Mr. Bailey. Until he had a son he trained to be as good as he was, maybe better.

Dropped out of sight.

CHAPTER 66

On the Road, Again

Billy figured taking Bobby out on the road would be just like having his own kid with him.

He didn't realize, though, that Bobby could brood sometimes, be moody, and give him the silent treatment.

Bobby just didn't know what to say to Billy. Billy, the experienced scout, the retired major leaguer. Billy, the husband and father. Billy, the friend of Yogi Berra. Billy, the easy-going, back-slapping guy who was essentially his trainer and chauffeur.

"So, Bobby, tell me a little about what you did as a player," Billy asked. "I hear you were a pitcher."

"Yup. Yup. Yup," Bobby replied. "I mostly pitched in relief. I wanted to start, but they had too many starters, so they put me in the 'pen. Mostly middle relief. Set-up. In high school, before I got drafted, I was a starter. Had a pretty good ERA—around high two. I was a good hitter, too, in high school. Always batted around 300. Liked going to the plate. Liked stealing bases. Liked running…"

"So…What was your bread-and-butter pitch? Fast ball? Curve?"

"Mostly fast ball. Cesar Dominguez—he was our pitching coach, up there in Jamestown—he was helping me develop a curve that broke inside and out. When I got up there my first year, my curve only broke inside, so the left-handed batters were having a field day with it."

"That Cesar! He was quite the pitcher in his day! And a very nice guy, I might add," Billy said.

Billy thinks everyone he met in baseball was a nice guy. No one was ever mean to him. In Billy's baseball memoir, no one will ever swear, chew tobacco, spit, throw at a batter, charge the mound, and no umpire will ever have made a bad call.

"That's what I hear," Bobby said.

"Hey, Billy, you know anyone on the Red Sox? Someone I played with in Jamestown is in trouble in Boston, and I thought if you knew anyone in Boston, they might be able to help him out. He's in jail, awaiting trial. At least, that's what I heard from one of the other teammates."

So maybe that's what's eating him up.

"What's the story, Bobby? What's this guy's name?"

"Jimmy Bailey. He's another pitcher. He wouldn't hurt a fly. He was a reliever, too, so I watched him a lot when we spent time in the 'pen. I mean, I don't talk much, but I watch a lot. Actually, I hope that helps me when I'm scouting, if I ever get the Mets approval to do it on my own."

Billy chuckled at this.

Bobby told Billy the story of Jimmy's night at the beach.

"Where did you hear all this, Bobby?"

"Jimmy wrote me a letter, but mostly from my friend Bud, who jumped way up from Jamestown to Triple-A in Memphis. He's been in contact with Jimmy's sister in Boston. I guess he's got a good lawyer, but they're running into a lot of roadblocks. That's what Bud says.

"And here's a good one for you, Billy. Do you know the Red Sox pitcher, Bill Lee?"

"The Spaceman? I know *of* him," Billy said.

"Well, out of the blue, he went to see Jimmy in jail. Seems he read about the case in the newspaper, and he drove down to the jail to visit him. Just told him to hang in, not to give up."

"Ain't that somethin'?" Billy said. "Well, I'd say that Jimmy already has some help from the Red Sox. I don't know anyone there. I think my wife may know Jean Yawkey, though. I'll ask her."

"Who's Jean Yawkey?" Bobby asked.

"She's married to the owner of the Red Sox, Tom Yawkey," Billy explained.

"Anything we could do would be great," Bobby said. "I feel so helpless."

Billy pulled into a motel called The Starlight.

"We're here for the night," he announced. Here is our Ritz on the road."

They were in Carlisle, Pennsylvania.

The Starlight was on the Mets' dime.

It would do.

CHAPTER 67

Sanity

D r. Beacon finally says I'm sane enough to stand trial.

I'm waiting for Joel so we can talk and figure this out.

I want to know if this means that the Massachusetts Department of Corrections will send me to a different prison, or if I will be staying here until the actual trial date.

The guard puts the key into the cell door. "Your lawyer's here. C'mon, get out. I don't have much time for this."

We walk to the encounter room. Joel is waiting.

"Jimmy, right now, I've got the assistant district attorney convinced to charge you with involuntary manslaughter instead of manslaughter, because it's a lighter sentence. I could go to speak to him about a plea bargain."

"But Joel, I didn't do it! I could see pleading to assault because I did fight with the guy, but I didn't throw him into the water."

"Jimmy, we don't have evidence. We need proof."

"Can't we bring in character witnesses who would testify that I wouldn't kill anyone?" I ask.

"With character witnesses, you're walking a very fine line," he explains. "For example, did you ever lose your temper in public?"

"Not that I can remember."

"Someone out there can probably remember. My point is, I can bring in your coach from Jamestown who would say that you were very patient and had good character, and the people whose home you stayed in while you were playing up there, and your roommate, and some of your high school teachers who would vouch for your character. Then somehow the DA would find someone in the town who would remember that one time that you blew your stack, and then all of a sudden, you're someone with a short fuse. Character assassination, it's called.

"I think our only chance is to go to the judge and the DA and see if we can get a plea bargain. You're not even 20 years old now, Jimmy. We might be able to get you a couple of years for this, and you'd come out and maybe be able to get back into baseball."

"A couple of years? How will I survive in prison?"

"The question is," Joel explains, ignoring me, "can we get the DA and the judge to even entertain this notion of a plea bargain? The DA seems to want to make an example out of you—high-profile athlete, known all over the region, gets into a fight, someone ends up dead. At least I was able to get them to agree to manslaughter.

"But Jimmy…I need your permission to negotiate with them further, to see if I can get them to offer a plea. Can I get your permission?"

My permission? My permission to go to jail for a crime I didn't do? My permission to devastate my family, and especially my father?

"So you see no other way, Joel? None at all?"

"I've been practicing criminal defense law for almost 20 years, and I've never run into a case like this one."

"Then I guess I have no choice but to give you my permission to negotiate and try to get me the best deal you can, Joel.

"Okay. All I can ask is that you do your best."

"I promise I will, Jimmy."

He knocks on the door, and the guard lets him out. I stand up, and the guard on the other side of the door takes me down the hallway, back to my cell.

I sit on the stiff mattress.

What I wouldn't give to walk into an empty ballpark and throw a few pitches to Russ and look up to find empty seats.

Peace and quiet.

Pitch and catch.

Empty seats.

CHAPTER 68

Memphis Rocks

The sweat never stopped dripping down Bud's face, arms and back, but his mind was focused only on pitching whenever he got the call from the bullpen.

Here in Memphis, he wasn't a starter. They used him for middle relief, and he was a great set-up man for their closer, Kenny Morano. The starting rotation was solid, and the home office seemed impressed by everyone's pitching.

Bud's goal was to get back to being a starter, but he was patient.

He was a team leader in Jamestown; in Memphis, he kept more to himself.

Morano was the one who got things done in this clubhouse, so Bud took his cues from Kenny. He had no idea how Kenny could withstand the heat, since he came from New Hampshire, but somehow, when Kenny was called in to close out a game, he was lights-out. He had a 1.92 ERA and averaged 1.2 strikeouts per inning. He was 6'5" but only weighed around 175 pounds. He stared down batters with his steely gaze, stacking up outs to end a game.

Bud's curiosity about people and places was a good fit for playing ball on the road. He loved hearing about the places where the guys had lived.

He still thought about Jimmy, doing time for something he didn't do.

Whenever Bud would get a letter from Jimmy, he wrote back immediately. Jimmy's sister Debbie sent newspaper clippings to help him keep up with the case.

She wrote to Bud, "Jimmy's signing bonus is gone. It's killing our dad. Our mother watches soap operas on TV all day. I think she figures that the people on the soap operas have bigger troubles than hers."

Here I sit, in sweaty Memphis, fulfilling my dream, while Jimmy waits to let a judge and jury determine his fate.

Bobby's somewhere looking at prospects; Jimmy has none.

CHAPTER 69

The Plea

"Joel, what's going on?"

He plunks down hard onto the chair on the other side of the table.

"Jimmy, I spoke to the judge and the DA about a plea. The DA still wants to make an example out of you, since he considers you a high-profile offender. He's recommended voluntary manslaughter instead of involuntary manslaughter, which carries a longer sentence. The judge said he's willing to listen to his reasoning. I presented all our information.

"The judge took notes during both the DA's presentation and mine. I couldn't read his facial expressions. It's up to him to decide whether the plea bargain will be for involuntary or voluntary manslaughter.

"But Jimmy...I want you to know that we presented the best case possible, having no evidence and no reliable witnesses."

"Did Dr. Beacon say I was sane enough to stand trial?"

"We're trying to avoid a trial, Jimmy, but yes, he did," Joel said. "I don't want to put you or your family through a trial."

"Okay, Joel. I have a lot to think about. Go do your job."

"Are you throwing me out? I'm doing my best here, Jimmy."

"No, no, that's not what I mean. I'm just angry and confused about having to go to jail for something I didn't do, and why the law doesn't protect the innocent. I could accept going to jail for assault, because I *did* do that, but not for manslaughter."

I see by the look on his face that he's disappointed in himself. And in me. But it's the law that let me down.

And I couldn't leave that beer alone when Paulie Donovan told me I couldn't have it that night.

CHAPTER 70

Prospecting for Gold

Billy had taken his seat on one of the lower bleacher rungs so he and Bobby would be on the same level. They were in Carlisle to watch a Connie Mack game, where a couple of talented young guys were pitching against each other.

Billy said these two young guys had been overlooked by other scouts in the past.

One of the pitchers, Danny O'Brien, was warming up on the sidelines. Bobby wondered if he knew he was being watched. Maybe the wheelchair could be a decoy.

The other, Brian Orlando, was tanned and thick around the waist. He did a little shoulder raise between pitches. He had his routine down pat.

Brian looked over at Bobby in the wheelchair.

Billy leaned down and said, "Hey, Bobby, that kid may have figured out why we're here. Let's go to the concession stand. We'll watch him from over there."

Brian kept tossing to the catcher, waiting for the game to begin.

Billy and Bobby kept an eye on Brian as he pitched four solid innings. He had a decent curve ball, and his fast ball had good velocity and went exactly where the catcher called it.

He seems pretty solid to me. Doesn't seem too flappable.

In the fifth inning, Brian gave up a lead-off triple, but he pitched his way out of it.

But Danny seemed nervous when he pitched, although he pitched well. His fast ball was popping into the catcher's mitt, and he struck out the first four batters.

In the top of the fifth, Danny gave up a home run over the centerfield fence, and he sat down on the mound for about ten seconds. When he got up, he quickly ended the inning with a strikeout.

Brian's team now led, 1–0.

This pitcher's duel went on through the eighth, and then the respective managers pulled Brian and Danny, and brought in the bullpen, turning the game into a free-for-all.

In the end, Brian's team won, 7–5.

"So, what did you think?" Billy asked Bobby.

"They're both consistent, both very different. Danny has a chicken dance on the mound, but he has a better fastball with more velocity. Brian has more poise and control. Fastball isn't as quick and doesn't have as much 'pop,' but it goes where the catcher asks for it."

"Good observations. I think both of them are coachable. Danny seems to be more anxious. Brian seems to be more of a natural athlete. Danny needs to put some meat on those bones. And learn how to relax.

"All our visits won't be this cut-and-dried, Bobby. This one was an easy one. Whaddya say we get some lunch? And not concession-stand hot dogs!"

CHAPTER 71

Road Warriors

They had some success in finding raw talent, like with the two Connie Mack pitchers, but they also saw some pretty bad baseball in search of what Billy called "diamonds in the rough."

"Hey, Billy, we're seeing more rough than diamonds these days."

"You're right, Bobby, you need to learn patience, my young friend. Satchel Paige used to look batters up and down and see if they 'possessed patience.' That's what we're doing. We're possessing patience."

Billy was not just teaching Bobby about evaluating baseball talent; he was also showing him how to ratchet down his own anxiety.

"Relax, kid, we'll get there when we get there. We've got a map, it's a nice day, and we're getting paid to do this. Imagine that, Bobby! We get paid to watch baseball! Ain't that a kick?"

Bobby sat back in the passenger seat as Billy drove, taking in the scenery. Cows. Horses. Cornfields. Sheep. Rolls of hay. More cows. Bobby was the keeper of the maps, although before this job, he had no idea how to read one. Billy had shown him that skill as well. This on-the-road experience made him wish he'd paid more attention in school.

All I cared about then was baseball. The teachers looked the other way because I was the star on the team. Billy's now teaching me things I should have learned in school. Or from my mom. My dad was useless because he wasn't there.

Common sense, too. I never learned any of that, either. I was too busy fighting with my mother and the notion of my father.

"Hey, Billy, what would you have been in you didn't go into baseball? I mean, like, would you have become an engineer or an architect or what?"

"Hmmmm....I haven't thought about that for a long time," Billy replied.

"My father was a farmer in Missouri, and I knew for damned sure that I didn't want to do *that*," he laughed. "I thought about going to college, but then I got signed to play baseball, and then I went into the Army during World War II. I was lucky I enlisted at the tail end of the war, so I didn't even leave the continental U.S. I just finished basic training and was getting ready to be shipped out when the war ended.

"I finished my time in the Army and then got back in touch with the Braves. They were still in Boston back then. They said they'd take me back. I felt like I was on cloud nine. They sent me back to the minors, and I was happier than a clam at high tide, let me tell you!

"Any thoughts I had about becoming a mechanic or a plumber or anything else just flipped away on the day I went to Braves Field in Boston, and I met the great lefthander Warren Spahn. My God, Bobby, that guy! He was so amazing. Such a nice guy and an incredible pitcher. He had a high leg kick, and when he let go the ball...Wow! And I was a rookie, just up from the minors, and he put his arm around me, and said, 'Kid, you're gonna be good, I just know it.' I will never forget the day he said that to me."

Just like the way Bud tried to put his arm around the guys in Jamestown. I never let him touch me. Never let him put his arm around me. Maybe he wanted to tell me I was gonna be good. Just like Warren Spahn told Billy. I'll never know.

"Then I met my wife Laura in Boston, and I was a marked man, you know?" Billy laughed. "Laura had me wrapped around her finger. I loved baseball, but I loved that woman even more. She stood by me all through my baseball career. She's an amazing woman."

"You know, Billy, one of the guys I played with up in Jamestown, his dad played ball right after the war, and his mother made his dad quit baseball. She made him choose between her and baseball. Would you ever think of quitting baseball for a woman?"

"So was that what happened to Jimmy Bailey's dad?"

"Yeah. That's what I heard."

"Yeah, I remember him. He was good, damned good. What a shame that he never pitched in the bigs," Billy said. "Rumor had it that he was being brought up from the minors, and all of a sudden, he just disappeared. That explains it.

"Laura loved baseball, too. She would never have asked me to give it up. I learned a lot of stuff from Laura. She's just one of the best ever made." He laughed again.

"Then I guess I'd better find me a Laura look-a-like," Bobby said. "Wanna marry me off to one of your daughters?"

"How big a dowry you willing to pay?" They both laughed as they pulled into a diner for lunch. "You buyin' today? That could be your first installment on that dowry."

CHAPTER 72

The Plea

T he clothes Joel sent for me are a little baggy. I've lost some weight since I've been in here.

The guard comes in and puts shackles on my hands and feet. We go outside, and the sun is almost unbearable. He leads me to the back of a van and locks me inside. The back end smells of sweat. When we arrive at the courthouse, he walks me up the steps where Joel is waiting.

The DA and the judge are waiting in the judge's chambers.

Joel holds my elbow as I shuffle in, restrained by the shackles.

I look down at the floor.

"Mr. Bailey, do you understand why you're here?" the judge asks.

"Yes, sir, I do," I reply.

"Your attorney has indicated that you are willing to accept a plea concerning the crime with which you have been charged. Do you understand the terms of this plea?"

"Yes, sir, I do."

"I have taken into advisement the arguments from the district attorney, as well as from your own defense attorney. The charge has been degraded from voluntary manslaughter to involuntary manslaughter.

"Do you have anything you would like to tell the court?"

"Yes, sir, your honor, I do."

"What say you?"

"I would like to thank you for considering my case. I would also like to go on record as saying that I am not guilty of killing that man. I did have a physical fight with him, but I did not kill him. But I cannot prove that. So on the advice of my lawyer, I have decided to accept this plea," I say.

What I want to say is, "I do not want to go to jail, please, your honor, don't send me to prison!"

"While I appreciate your statement, Mr. Bailey, I must follow the letter of the law. Therefore, on the count of involuntary manslaughter, I hereby sentence you to four to six years in the Walpole State Prison, with credit for time served. I will waive any assault charges that may have been lodged against you."

Four to six years? With credit for time served, the earliest I could get out would be when I'm 22.

Joel speaks up. "Thank you, your honor, we appreciate your consideration."

"Your honor, we ask that he be remanded immediately to Walpole State Prison," the DA says.

"No, I will give him the opportunity to return to Bridgewater to gather any belongings he may have. He will be remanded on Monday of next week," the judge says.

"May I have a word with my client, judge?" Joel asks.

"Certainly, Mr. Goldblum," the judge says.

"Jimmy, there's a possibility you will get out earlier, as long as you do everything you're supposed to do—good behavior.

"Walpole is a maximum security prison. You're gonna have to watch your back and figure out how to fit in."

"Joel, I am petrified," I say. "I feel so alone here."

"You have a lot of people pulling for you," he says. "Your sisters, your parents, your teammates. I even get calls about you from Bill Lee. And I'll keep in touch. I may come to visit you as well. I wish we had a different outcome, Jimmy. I did all I could."

CHAPTER 73

No Blues in Memphis

Bud struck out six in three innings, gave up no runs, walked one, and the other outs were easy infield plays. Then Kenny Morano came in and sewed it up.

Bud and Kenny were an outstanding one-two punch. Even though they were under contract with The Expos, Bud could tell that scouts from other teams were in the stands.

You never know when you're going to be traded. You never know if they're going to use you as bait for a hard-hitting center fielder or defensive catcher.

The players would look up from the dugout into the stands and see people they recognized as retired ballplayers, with little spiral-bound notebooks.

On the field, the players made every effort to ignore them, but the undercurrent remained. They were under baseball's microscope, and each little electron of their being would be analyzed. The game was their opportunity to show off their hearts and souls in ways they couldn't off the field.

This team had accepted Bud, even though he'd made that giant leap from Single-A to Triple-A ball. He and Kenny Murano hung around a little, and Bud spoke more freely about where he had come from, his school and family background.

He didn't smoke or drink, although many of the other guys did. Some of the guys called him "The Reverend." In fact, he often craved beer, especially in the heat. He just knew it would hamper his conditioning plan, and he refused to let that happen.

The Memphis Blues finished second in their division, and Arnie sat Bud down just before he returned to Vanderbilt.

"Kid, I just want you to know what a big part y'all played in our success this year," he told Bud. "Last year, we finished, well, dead last. A lot of our success comes from the way you and Kenny worked together. I'm expecting that the home club may want you to go to spring training next year. What're you gonna do if that happens? Take time off from college?"

"I don't really know, Arnie. I hadn't thought about it. But I will."

He pulled Bud toward him and gave him a bear hug.

"You got it, kid. You're gonna make it. I don't know if it'll be with this team or another one, but you're gonna make it. I can see it in the way you pitch, but I can also see it in your eyes."

Arnie says I'm gonna make it.

"Thanks, Arnie, I've had a great coach this year. This is a great team, too, nice group of guys. I appreciate what you've done for me," Bud replied.

"Bud, see you soon. Hoping on the mound in Montreal!"

"I'll practice my French, just for you!"

"Oooh la la!" Arnie laughed at him.

I love this guy.

CHAPTER 74

Walpole

Today's the day they're sending me to Walpole. As much as I hate this place, I don't know how I'll make it there. Maximum security. Joel says hardened criminals are there. Murderers. Rapists. Armed robbers. Gang members. Mafiosos. I'm only a former baseball player from Weymouth. I'm not as strong as I was when I was in training; I feel pretty weak.

The guard puts the key in the door and it creaks open. "Time to go," he says.

Down the hall we go, doors opening, doors slamming behind us, out into a van. This time, three other inmates are being transferred with me. Two are also white and the third is a very thin black guy with two teeth missing on the bottom. His eyes look like they're going to bug out of his head, kind of like a frog sitting on a lily pad, scanning for his next meal as insects fly over.

We're all wearing the same get-up—denim jumpsuits with black vertical stripes—the official "uniform" of Bridgewater State Prison. Maybe we'll get different clothes when we get to Walpole.

We all look petrified—blank stares on pale faces. Even the black guy's face looks ashen, as if the blood has left his brain. No one speaks, but each shows his nervousness in his own way. One is biting his fingernails, while another is pulling at his ear. The black guy is twirling his closely cropped curly hair. I am hearing music in my head—"Take Me Out to the Ballgame." It stays with me for the entire drive, playing like a broken record, over and over in my head. I estimate it's about 30 miles from Bridgewater to Walpole.

We're all sitting on the bench seats, but we have no seat belts. We are constrained by handcuffs and leg shackles, secured by a chain that binds those together. We're not able to move around much, but every time the van hits a bump, we fly upward and sideways, often hitting our heads or parts of our bodies on the insides of the van. None of us can stop from bouncing around. Whenever we hit a part of the van, we make eye contact, but none of us asks if one of the others is hurt.

We feel the van slow down and hear a gate swing open. *We must have arrived. I'm not ready for this. I'm sure none of these other guys are, either. My stomach is a mess. My head is aching. "Root, root, root for the home team, if they don't win, it's a shame..."*

We hear a lot of commotion on the outside as the van stops. The back end opens, and the guard yells, "Sit down! Don't move! Any of you!"

We all look down at the floor of the van. I realize I have numerous bruises all over my body from bouncing around the back of the vehicle. I also realize it would do no good to tell anyone about it, no good to complain. I'll have to live with these bruises until they go away. Or until they're replaced by new bruises. Or worse.

The guard has a clipboard in his hand. He's talking to another guard. They're going over names. I hear my name mentioned. They glance back at the van, then move on. The two of them come to the door and tell us to get out. But none of us can move right. We try to get out, but it's more like falling out.

Standing behind the fences are the other inmates. They're looking at us like we're pieces of meat being brought in. Lambs to the slaughter. They're hooting and hollering and making rude remarks about, shall we say, our physical appearance. The skinny black guy is getting lots of comments.

Apparently my face is pretty bruised because I hear someone yell out, "Hey, that guy—the blonde—who worked him over?" Then everyone laughs.

One of the other guys who had been in the van with me turned around and says under his breath, "They're talking about you, man. Your face looks like you just came out of a fight, like someone's been punchin' your face. Must've happened when we were bouncin' around that van."

The four of us walk in and go through processing. They take our weight, height, and make us strip. We get new clothes, too—denim shirts and blue jeans, neither of which fit me or any of the others who came in with me. We each get four sets of underwear and socks, a toothbrush, toothpaste, and shaving cream, courtesy of the Commonwealth of Massachusetts

Department of Corrections, and learn that we will earn laundry privileges and spending money through the jobs we are assigned within the prison. They do not issue razors or razorblades to us. We must be supervised when shaving, according to the person who is doing our orientation.

"Now, I know you guys are all a little off your rockers, coming from Bridgewater and all," he says. "So you probably didn't have razors or razorblades there, neither. But here it's even more critical that you not have access to razors or razorblades. You understand?"

We look at him and nod.

"You will all share a cell with someone. You will all be assigned a job. We have strict rules about visitors. You get one phone call per week, ten minutes, and it's got to be made collect to whoever you're calling. If the call gets disconnected in the middle, tough shit. You have to wait for the next week.

"Your job allows you to earn stamps. No one from the outside can bring postage stamps in. If you get caught with contraband, you go in the hole—solitary confinement. How long depends on what the contraband is. Or how the guard who puts you there feels like keeping you there.

"We got other rules, and sometimes we make up new ones as we go along. If you don't like the rules, tough shit. And don't ever, ever, ever think of going to the warden to complain, or having one of your outsider friends write the warden a letter to complain. That don't go over so good.

"Now, I'm supposed to ask if you have any questions, but I don't wanna hear any questions."

He looks at the guards in the back, snaps his fingers, and they come to get the four of us. He snaps his fingers again, and somehow we all know we need to stand up. The guards take us out into the hallway. Most of the inmates are back in their cells. They're screaming at us, but I can't understand what they're saying. The noise level here makes what we had at Bridgewater seem tame by comparison. It echoes off the tiers of iron-barred cells as if it were some sort of bizarre concrete Grand Canyon, or even like the Quincy Quarry, where guys go to jump into the water from great height. Before they jump, they yell, and I used to think that echo was loud.

That was before I got *here*.

I've never heard noise like this. I mean, when the Beatles played Wonderland dog park, no one could hear the music because the girls were screaming. High-pitched, shrill screams. Blood-curdling screams. But what

I'm hearing today feels like dark, foreboding threats. Alfred Hitchcock movies. *Psycho*. The birds attacking Tippi Hedrin. She had nowhere she could escape.

I can't escape, either.

I'm completely unprotected, a knight without armor, a Christian facing the lions in the Coliseum, an astronaut without a space suit, a trapeze artist without a net, a bullfighter without a cape, a person who didn't commit a crime facing a firing squad. I've got nothing.

They put me and the black guy in the same empty cell and the other two from Bridgewater in an empty cell across from us. All four of us look like deer in the headlights on a cold fall night.

The black guy tells me his name is Keeshon, and he's from Dorchester. I can't hear anything else he says to me. The decibel level is uncontrollable, and my head, ears and entire body hurts. I yell my name back to him, and he says he can remember it. We nod back at one another.

We fold our clothes and stack them near our cots. The mattresses are slightly better than they were at Bridgewater, but not much.

How the hell does anyone get any sleep around this place? If the inmates are all keyed up, maybe it's because they're sleep-deprived. How will I survive for the next four to six years?

I hear a key unlock our cell.

"Bailey, warden wants to see you."

What did I do now? Keeshon looks at me as if to say, "Don't leave me!"

The guard walks me past inmates who are hooting and hollering at us, so the guard takes his night stick and bangs on their cells. "Shaddup! All of you bums!"

The warden wears a navy-blue suit. He introduces himself as Eli Manfred.

"Sit down, Jimmy. I know you just arrived here, and it's never an easy transition for inmates to come here from Bridgewater." He rings the buzzer on his desk. "Charlotte, will you ask our visitors to come in, please?"

The door behind me opens again.

Much to my surprise, in walk Debbie, Donna and Joel. Debbie and Donna look like they've been crying.

"Jimmy, we have bad news for you," the warden says.

Donna is sobbing uncontrollably.

Debbie blurts out, "Dad killed himself last night!"

I can't think.

This *has* to be a nightmare.

Joel takes over.

"Jimmy, your dad left a suicide note. He shot himself in the chest. He did this in a little shed behind your house. Your mother heard the noise and found him."

My dad? Dead? Suicide? The shed?

"It's all your fault!" Donna blurts out. "He said he couldn't live anymore, knowing you're in this place, that you blew everything by killing that guy!"

Why couldn't he believe me?

"Donna, I took the plea because I had no one to back me up, no witnesses, no evidence..."

"I tried to explain it to Dad, Joel tried to explain it to him, but he wouldn't believe either one of us," I say. "Oh, my God, oh, my God, oh, my God..."

I can hear them all talking in the room, but I don't know what they're saying.

I see Dad and me, near that shed, in the backyard, tossing a ball back and forth, playing with Pepe, Dad showing me how to throw a curve ball, Dad with me when I earned my first trophy for outstanding Little Leaguer, for best high school player in Massachusetts, and on the day The Expos drafted me.

Dad, putting his arm around me, so proud of everything I'd—we'd—accomplished on the ballfield. Dad, walking around the field with me in Jamestown. Dad's fat fingers, worn to the bone, working at the shipyard, so that Debbie, Donna and I could live our dreams.

"Jimmy, are you listening?" Joel asks.

"We're trying to figure out how to get you released for a few hours so you can attend the funeral. The warden is trying to work something out. He would have to send you with a few guards, and you'd have to go in chains. Can you handle that?" Joel asks.

"I guess I can. But Joel, it's all my fault that he did this."

"No, Jimmy. When someone's suicidal, they're mentally ill," the warden explains. "Your dad would have eventually done this, whether or not you came here."

And Dad would never talk to anyone about things that bothered him. Never.

"How's mom holding up?" I ask.

"Not well," Debbie says, wiping her eyes. "but she has some good friends, and they will help her through it."

My dad killed himself and said it's my fault. He was convinced I killed that guy and that made him not want to live anymore. Again, I hear them all talking in the room. The warden is on the phone. He makes several calls, one right after another.

I don't know what's going on. I don't know how I'll make it through another day, in a cell, thinking about my dad and what he thought about in the last second of his life.

CHAPTER 75

The Letter

Bud returned to Vanderbilt feeling more confident about his chances for success in baseball, but he wanted to continue his path toward earning a degree in biology/pre-med, his Plan B.

He hadn't heard from Jimmy for a while.

Bobby called him often, usually from the road, just to check in.

"I'm the rolling scoutmaster," he told Bud. "No one suspects because I'm in the chair. I'm like a baseball sleuth."

Six weeks into the first semester, he got a letter from Jimmy, with a different return address this time, a place in Massachusetts called MCI Walpole.

Dear Bud,

Well, it's been a while since I wrote to you. I hope your school is going good for you.

I have a lot of news, most of it bad. My lawyer advised me to take a plea bargain because we could not find any witnesses or evidence to support my innocence. So I took the plea, and I'll probably be here in Walpole State Prison for up to six years. It's a terrible place. My lawyer says maybe I could get out early for good behavior.

My dad is dead. He committed suicide. He did it on the day they sent me to this place. He said in the note that he had nothing else to live for because I wouldn't ever play baseball again. I tried to explain to him that if I got out of jail in four to five years, maybe The Expos would give me another chance. My lawyer told him the same thing. I guess he didn't believe either one of us.

My mother's a mess. My two sisters blame me. I got to attend my dad's funeral. I had to be escorted by two guards and wear an orange jumpsuit, with handcuffs and leg shackles and a chain connecting the two, to the church.

I can't get it out of my mind that it probably WAS my fault, at least, mostly my fault.

Can you send me a letter that has some good news in it? I need it.

Your friend,

Jimmy

Bud was shocked.

This news came to Bud on the same day he heard from The Expos.

He was invited to spring training in February.

He'd be taking next semester off.

His plan seemed to be the only one that had stayed an A.

CHAPTER 76

In Common

After a year, Keeshon and I continue to share a cell. He's quiet and the crime that led to his being sent here was kind of like mine. He took money from an old lady he was helping take care of, and he swears that she told him he could have it. The old lady's family said that she wasn't of her right mind, so she couldn't have given him permission. They prosecuted him. He still insists that she gave him the money. You know what? I believe him, knowing what I went through. But they gave him eight years. Eight years! He had a public defender, while I had Joel. What a difference a good lawyer makes.

He and I tell each other stories about what our lives were like before we got here. He had two little sisters and one older brother. His father was a driver for the MBTA and was killed in an accident. His mother was left to raise the kids on her own. She did the best she could, he says, but she had trouble putting food on the table, even after a settlement from the accident.

His older brother took to stealing food from local convenience stores until the owner of one of them gave him a job. Then things got better, because the owner would give the family expired food and fruit that was just about to go bad.

Keeshon was never very good in school, so I'm helping him get better at reading and writing. Now he likes to read; he says he didn't like it when he was in school.

CHAPTER 77

Jimmy

Three years have passed since my dad committed suicide.
Keeshon and I use up a lot of time telling tales and comparing our lives. It helps get through the days.

I tell him stories about my dad and The Filly. He loves my baseball memories. He can't believe I have a sister who graduated from Harvard.

I tell him about my friend Bud Prescott, who has made it to the bigs as a starting pitcher for The Montreal Expos. Bud's running an ERA just under 3.00, and he still can hit the ball, too.

Bud has a woman now. Her name is Kathy, and he plans to ask her to marry him later this year. He says he met her in Montreal. Bud's plan B of going to medical school to become a sports medicine doctor is on hold right now.

In his letters, Bobby says he meets women here and there but hasn't found anyone special.

I dream of different shades of green—emerald, jade, lime, pea green, seafoam, etc.—and put them together to envision the luxurious grasses in different baseball fields.

I try to summon the smell of newly-mown grass to cover up the damp, concrete, urine-soaked aromas that surround our cell.

I imagine the feel of a handful of coarse dirt from the mound, which I rub into the baseball in my other hand.

I look into the stands and I can see my dad, waving to me, as I get ready to pitch in today's game.

He's smiling, happy the coach has decided to put me in against our biggest rival.

I adjust my cap and look out from the mound and see Russ. He's giving me a signal for a curve ball. I shake him off. He agrees to a fastball.

My dad approves.

I throw a strike.

Acknowledgments

When I was growing up in North Weymouth, Massachusetts, my family members were not necessarily interested in baseball. Somehow, though, I became a Red Sox fan, in 1956, and remain one to this day.

My first compatriots who went to Red Sox games at Fenway Park were Elaine Chalet Sheeran, Charlotte Brunet and Claire Milmore MacDonald. My cousin Helen Brown Jalkut and I used to go to the Patriots' Day doubleheaders at Fenway, and most of the time, we were bundled up against the April cold and rain while people were running in the Boston Marathon. We had great times back then, and I appreciate the fact that they were always there, ready to take the two buses and two trains that it took to get from North Weymouth to Fenway.

I met Myrna Cohen Thurnher at the Sportsmens' Show in Boston, which we had gone to so that we could meet Ted Williams, and we also became baseball friends. It was through Myrna that I met Bill Fischer, at the Boston College coffeehouse, and he would ultimately become my husband in 1973. Amazing how those things work out.

I had wanted to be a sportswriter back in the 1960s, but Rick Reichardt of the then-California Angels, whom I met as he was walking back to Kenmore Square from Fenway one day, convinced me not to take that path, that it was too much of a glass ceiling to shatter at that time. He probably doesn't remember the letter he wrote to me explaining that, but I do. It's somewhere in the stuff my mother left me. Thanks, Rick.

Thanks to Kitty Sheehan for editing the final draft and for Ellen Toner for editing the first draft. And to Amy Collins for her encouragement throughout the process. You made all the difference.

Thanks to Herb Sweet for helping me with the New York Mets portion of the book. He knows all things Queens, NY.

Thanks to the Boston Red Sox, for winning the 2004, 2007 and 2013 World Series, and for bringing me the joys of winning and also teaching me how to lose during those many years in between. I am also grateful to the Red Sox for allowing me to serve as Fenway Park's public address announcer for one day in 2012 for a game between the Red Sox and Minnesota Twins. It was one of the most amazing days of my life, to work with John Carter, Jack Lanzillotti as producer, T.J. Connolly the Fenway Park DJ, and Josh Kantor, the Fenway Park organist. Jack's untimely accidental death two years later broke many hearts in Red Sox Nation. What a wonderful talent this world lost when Jack left us.

To Jim Rice, Dustin Pedroia, Mike Lowell, Pedro Martinez, and Mi Papi Grande, David Ortiz. They've kept my Red Sox spark alive for so many years. They don't know me, but I know them. Mi Papi Grande es mi corazon de béisbol.

Thanks to my teachers in the Weymouth school system. You gave me the foundation necessary to finish college as the first person in my family to do so. Specifically, Ed White, who always cautioned me that I had to "learn to walk before I could run." I never forgot.

Thanks to Jared Carrabis and his mother, Ellyn Welch Carrabis, whose wonderful family stays grounded in the real world while staying surrounded by baseball. Jared wrote a book a number of years ago, and I knew then he was going places. He has done just that. Remember the name.

Thanks to my grown-up children, Becky Prevost and Tim Fischer, and their spouses, John Prevost and Lynn Owin Fischer, for not making fun of me when I told them I'd written a novel. (What the world needs now is one more novel, right?) The grandchildren Liam, Lorene, John and Brendan will one day grow up and realize that they're all part of this as well.

My nieces, Sara and Whitney Troy, who became part of our nuclear family in 1997, should receive my thanks, too. My niece, Victoria Walsh, too, who has learned to love the "Boston Red Soxes."

My mother and father, Gertrude and Giles Adams, were both long deceased before I began this project. They put up with a lot of my passions, including baseball. I hope they're somehow able to realize that I finally did this.

To my folk music friends: You're all amazing, and I appreciate your encouragement throughout the process. So many of you are also baseball fans. We're always second-guessing the managers!

Thanks to my tennis friends, especially Donna Smith, who goes with me to Red Sox fan weekend every year, even though she's a Yankee fan. She puts up with a lot from me, vis-à-vis baseball.

And finally, to Bill Fischer, whom I completely surprised by handing him 200 pages of a preliminary draft of this manuscript and said, "Would you read this and tell me if I should continue writing this?": Thanks for working hard all those years as a physician and dedicating your life to people in need. Baseball is baseball, but medicine extends life. Thanks for reading my draft and telling me to continue. This is the result.

The characters in this book are fictional; my love for baseball is not. As I get older, the game remains something I look forward to every spring. Win or lose, Little League game or MLB, I simply love this game. Just like the people in this book.

Author Biography

Even though no one in her immediate family was a baseball fan, Wanda Adams Fischer became interested in the game when she was not quite eight years old, becoming a fan of the Boston Red Sox in 1956. She's remained a member of Red Sox Nation ever since.

Born in Kingsport, Tennessee and raised near Boston in Weymouth, Massachusetts, she began writing at a young age and had wanted to become a sportswriter. However, the turbulent 1960s got in the way, and instead tried her hand at radio news broadcasting after earning a degree in English from Northeastern University.

Ultimately, she left the news business for a nearly 40-year career in public relations/marketing/media relations in not-for-profit and government organizations, retiring from full-time work in 2014. The recipient of several awards during her career, she has been recognized by her peers for writing, editing, photography and marketing campaigns,

She still does on-air radio work, as host of "The Hudson River Sampler," a folk music program that debuted on September 18, 1982 on WAMC-FM/ Northeast Public Radio, a major National Public Radio affiliate in Albany, NY. She is also a singer and sometimes songwriter, and has produced a recording, "Singing Along with the Radio."

In 2012, she had the opportunity to sit in the public address announcer's chair at Fenway Park as the "guest in the chair" and announce a full Major League Baseball game between the Red Sox and the Minnesota Twins. She filled that role for a full nine innings, and notes that it was one of the biggest thrills of her life.

An avid competitive tennis player, she was part of a team that competed in the 2004 senior nationals in Palm Springs, finishing second in the nation at their level.

She's been married since 1973 to Bill Fischer; they have two grown children, Becky Fischer Prevost and Tim Fischer, and four grandchildren. Wanda and Bill live in Schenectady, New York.